POCKET BOOK
OF PRAYERS

POCKET BOOK OF PRAYERS

Selected with an Introduction by
M. Basil Pennington, O.C.S.O.

IMAGE BOOKS
A Division of Doubleday New York

OPM

Library of Congress Cataloging-in-Publication Data
Main entry under title:

Pocket book of prayers.

1. Prayers. I. Pennington, M. Basil.
BV245.P63   1986   242   85-12936
ISBN: 0-385-23298-5

This
Pocket Book of Prayers
is dedicated to
Saint Anne

"Ask her to help you to be faithful to the
interior life and a spirit of prayer."*

* This "word of life" was given to me by my spiritual father on the day I received the monastic cowl, the Feast of Saint Anne, 1953.

Contents

Introduction

We want to pray. But we don't know how. Saint Paul told us, with all the truth of the Sacred Scriptures: "We do not know how to pray as we ought." But he added: "But the Holy Spirit teaches us."

How does the Holy Spirit teach us to pray?

He teaches us in the deep quiet places of our heart—when we are quiet enough to listen. It is difficult for us to quiet down and listen. A simple method like Centering Prayer can start us on our way.

He teaches us through the Sacred Scriptures. Especially through the Gospels, but all of Scripture is written for our instruction. Scripture, of course, teaches us many things and the danger is that we will approach the Sacred Text primarily from an intellectual point of view, to learn rather than to pray. A simple method of Scripture Prayer can help us begin to listen to the Sacred Scriptures in such a way that this listening is part of a dialogue to which we respond. This is true prayer.

Both these methods will be found in this *Pocket Book of Prayers.*

The Holy Spirit also speaks to us through the Tradition—through other fellow travelers on the journey, those who have gone before and those of our own day, those who are well known and those who are known to God alone. In the case of many of the most beautiful prayers that have come down to us through the centuries, we do not know in whose heart the Spirit first uttered them. They are part of our common heritage. We are all one Body in Christ. They are, therefore, our prayers.

This little book offers many of these prayers. The difficulty has not been in finding suitable prayers to include in this pocket-sized book but rather in deciding which of the many prayers that have touched my life at different times on the journey should be included and which must be left aside in order to keep our book within proportions. It is a very personal selection. You might, for example, be surprised to find a prayer to Saint Francis Xavier. After all, I am not a Jesuit. But back in the days when I was searching to know God's will in my life, the arm of this great saint and missionary, the hand which baptized countless thousands and has been preserved by God's intervention, was brought to my diocese. My time in prayer in the presence of that sacred relic was one of those special moments in prayer that are engraved deeply in my spirit, never to be forgotten.

In this book you will find something old and something new, something (much) borrowed and something blue—if we take blue to signify Mary, the Virgin Mother of God, the universal Mediatrix, through whom all prayer flows up to the throne of her Divine Son, our one great Mediator with the Father.

The Church—and we are the Church—likes what is old not because it is old but because it is "young"—it goes back to her youth, to the *sources* of her life: the Sacred Scriptures and the Living Tradition. In prayers drawn from the Old Testament and from the Jewish tradition we use the very phrases used by Jesus in speaking to his Father. For this reason these prayers, especially the Psalms, have never ceased to be on the lips of his followers and disciples. We also use with predilection sentiments that were first uttered by him and by his Mother. Many other prayers are favorites because they have poured forth first from the pure hearts of his dearest friends, the saints, women and men who asked: "Lord, teach us how to pray," and who learned well what they were taught.

There are many different ways in which we can use these prayers:

We can simply say them, making their sentiments our own as best we can.

We can pray them more reflectively, pausing between the words and phrases, allowing them to open out in our hearts. We might soon find ourselves branching out and praying in our own words. Good! Our mentor would be only too happy. And our Lord even happier. He loves the lisping of his children, as well as the more sophisticated poetics or prose of his less simple ones—just so long as we do not get caught up in our own performance and forget to whom we are talking.

We can use a particular prayer or the phrases of a litany as the subject matter of meditation, searching more deeply into the meaning, placing the mystery into context. After our musings, our imagining, our pondering, we will probably be ready to pray the prayer as much more our own. Or go on to pray in our own words. Or just settle into silent, loving communion with the Lord in the heart of the mystery.

Again, we may take a phrase of one of the prayers or one of the brief prayers found in the last section and carry it with us through the day. We may repeat it in our minds or on our lips. Gradually it will sink down into our hearts, and become a prayer of the heart. We may find it is the response to some or many of the things that come up in that day. If each day one of these words of life forms our mind and heart, we will quickly come to have the "mind of Christ." This is one of the ways we come to that continual prayer, that praying without ceasing, which was commanded of us by the Lord and by his apostle, Paul.

As we pray, we are, of course, conscious of God and enter into communion with him. Sometimes we also address ourselves to his holy Mother or another of his friends. But whether we advert to it or not—and at times it can be very helpful deliberately to advert to it—we are always praying in communion with a mighty host of pray-ers: those who first used these prayers and all those who have used them through the centuries: Jesus, Mary and Joseph, David, Solomon and Jonathan, Peter, Paul and John the Beloved Disciple, Augustine, Basil and his friend Gregory, Benedict, Bernard and Bruno, Dominic, Clare and Francis, Teresa, John and Ignatius, and the saints and martyrs of our own day, Oscar Romero, Teresa of Calcutta, and Jean Donovan of Chicago. We do not pray alone. Above all, the Spirit of God, who has been given to us and has become our Spirit, prays deep within us with his unutterable outpourings of love. Never need we fear the poverty of our prayer, our distraction, our empty heads and dry hearts. When we pray we do not pray alone. All the fullness of the Divine Love always prays with us.

Fr. M. Basil, O.C.S.O.

Saint Joseph's Abbey, Spencer
Lent, 1985

POCKET BOOK
OF PRAYERS

1

Prayers for Every Day

BASIC PRAYERS

The Sign of the Cross

In the Name of the Father, and of the Son, and of the Holy Spirit. Amen.

The Lord's Prayer

Our Father, who art in heaven, hallowed be thy Name. Thy kingdom come. Thy will be done on earth as it is in heaven. Give us this day our daily bread. And forgive us our trespasses as we forgive those who trespass against us. And lead us not into temptation but deliver us from evil.

For thine is the kingdom and the power and the glory now and forever.

Amen.

The Angelic Salutation

Hail Mary, full of grace, the Lord is with you. Blessed are you among women. And blessed is the fruit of your womb, Jesus. Holy Mary, Mother of God, pray for us sinners, now and at the hour of our death. Amen.

The Doxology

Glory be to the Father, and to the Son, and to the Holy Spirit, as it was in the beginning, is now, and ever shall be, world without end. Amen.

An Act of Faith

O my God, I firmly believe that you are one God in three divine Persons, Father, Son, and Holy Spirit. I believe that your divine Son became man and died for our sins and that he will come to judge the living and the dead. I believe these and all the truths which you have revealed, because you have revealed them, you who can neither deceive nor be deceived.

An Act of Hope

O my God, relying on your infinite goodness and promises, I hope to obtain pardon of my sins, the help of your grace, and life everlasting through the merits of Jesus Christ, my Lord and Redeemer. Amen.

An Act of Love

O my God, I love you above all things with my whole heart and soul because you are all-good and worthy of all my love. I love my neighbor as myself for love of you. I forgive all who have offended me and I ask pardon of all whom I have offended. Amen.

MORNING PRAYERS

Blessed be the Name of the Lord, from this time forth and forevermore.

From the rising of the sun to its setting, the Name of the Lord is to be praised.

The Morning Offering

O Jesus, through the Immaculate Heart of Mary, I offer you all my prayers, works, joys, and suffering of this day for all the intentions of your Sacred Heart, in union with the Holy Sacrifice of the Mass throughout the world, in reparation for my sins, for the intentions of all our associates, and in particular for the special intention of this month [determined by the Holy Father]. Amen.

The Serenity Prayer

God grant me
  serenity to accept the things I cannot
    change,
  courage to change the things I can,
    and
  wisdom to know the difference.

The Canticle of Zachary

(The *Benedictus*)

Blessed be the Lord, the God of Israel,
for he has visited his people, he has come
    to their rescue

and has raised up for us a power of
    salvation
in the house of his servant David;
even as he proclaimed,
by the mouth of his holy prophets from
    ancient times,
that he would save us from our
    enemies
and from the hands of all who hate us.
Thus he shows mercy to our ancestors,
thus he remembers his holy covenant;
the oath he swore
to our father Abraham
that he would grant us, free from fear,
to be delivered from the hands of our
    enemies,
to serve him in holiness and virtue
in his presence, all our days.
And you, little child,
you shall be called prophet of the Most
    High,
for you will go before the Lord
to prepare the way for him,
to give his people knowledge of
    salvation
through the forgiveness of their sins;
this by the tender mercy of our God
who from on high will bring the rising
    Sun to visit us,
to give light to those who live
in darkness and the shadow of death,

and to guide our feet
into the way of peace.
Glory be to the Father, and to the Son,
and to the Holy Spirit,
as it was in the beginning, is now,
and ever shall be, world without end.
    Amen.

—Luke 1:68–79

Prayer to Our Guardian Angel

Angel of God, my guardian dear,
to whom his love commits me here,
ever this day be at my side,
to watch, to lead, to guard, to guide.

THE CREEDS

The Apostles' Creed

I believe in God, the Father Almighty, Creator of heaven and earth, and in Jesus Christ, his only Son, our Lord, who was conceived by the Holy Spirit, born of the Virgin Mary, suffered under Pontius Pilate, was crucified, died, and was buried. He descended into hell, the third day he rose from the dead. He ascended into heaven and sits on the right hand of God the Father Almighty. From

thence he shall come to judge the living
and the dead. I believe in the Holy Spirit,
the holy Catholic Church, the communion of saints, the forgiveness of sins, the
resurrection of the body, and life everlasting. Amen.

The Nicene Creed

(The Credo)

We believe in one God, the Father,
the Almighty, Maker of heaven and
earth, of all that is seen and unseen. We
believe in one Lord, Jesus Christ, the only
Son of God, eternally begotten of the Father, God from God, Light from Light,
true God from true God, begotten, not
made, one in Being with the Father.
Through him all things were made. For
us and for our salvation he came down
from heaven. By the power of the Holy
Spirit he was born of the Virgin Mary and
became man. For our sakes he was crucified under Pontius Pilate; he suffered,
died, and was buried. On the third day he
rose again in fulfillment of the Scriptures.
He ascended into heaven and is seated at
the right hand of the Father. He will
come again in glory to judge the living
and the dead, and his kingdom will have

no end. We believe in the Holy Spirit, the Lord, the giver of life, who proceeds from the Father and the Son. With the Father and the Son he is worshiped and glorified. He has spoken through the Prophets. We believe in one, holy, catholic, and apostolic Church. We acknowledge one baptism for the forgiveness of sins. We look for the resurrection of the body and the life of the world to come. Amen.

THE ANGELUS

The angel of the Lord declared unto Mary, and she conceived of the Holy Spirit.
Hail, Mary. . . .
Behold the handmaid of the Lord,
be it done unto me according to your word.
Hail, Mary. . . .
The Word was made Flesh,
and dwelt among us.
Hail, Mary. . . .
Pray for us, O holy Mother of God,
that we may be made worthy of the
   promises of Christ.
Let us pray.

Pour forth, we beseech you, O Lord, your grace into our hearts, that we to whom the Incarnation of your divine Son was made known by the message of an angel may by his Passion and Cross be brought to the glory of his Resurrection, who lives and reigns forever and ever. Amen.

QUEEN OF HEAVEN

(The *Regina coeli*)

(This is said in place of the *Angelus* during the Paschaltime)

Queen of heaven, rejoice, alleluia,
for he whom you did deserve to bear, alleluia,
has risen as he said, alleluia.
Pray for us to God, alleluia.
Rejoice and be glad, O Virgin Mary, alleluia,
for the Lord is truly risen, alleluia.
Let us pray.

O God, who by the Resurrection of your Son, our Lord Jesus Christ, have vouch-safed to give joy to the whole world, grant, we beseech you, that through the intercession of the Virgin Mary, his Mother, we may attain the joys of eternal life. We ask this through Christ, our Lord. Amen.

GRACE BEFORE MEALS

Bless us, O Lord, and these your gifts, which we are about to receive from your bounty, through Christ, our Lord, and his Immaculate Mother. Amen.

* * *

Blessed are you, Lord, God of all creation, through your goodness we have this food to eat, which earth has given and human hands have made. May it sustain us for eternal life. Amen.

* * *

Blessed are you, Lord, our God, King of the universe, who nourishes the entire world; in your goodness, with grace, with loving kindness, and with mercy, you give nourishment to all flesh, for your loving kindness is eternal. Through your great goodness, nourishment was never lacking to us and may it never be lacking to us forever, for the sake of your Great Name, because you are the God who nourishes and sustains all and benefits all and prepares food for all of your creatures which you have created. As it is said, "You open your hand and satisfy the desire of every living thing." Blessed are you, Lord, who nourishes all.

—from the Jewish tradition

*   *   *

Father, bless us and bless our food; bless all those who make it possible for us to enjoy your gifts. And, Father, we pray, too, for our hungry sisters and brothers everywhere. Teach us so to share so that no one will hunger on this your bountiful earth. Amen.

*   *   *

Good food,
good meat,
good God, let us eat. Amen.

THANKSGIVING AFTER MEALS

We thank you, O Lord, for these your gifts which we have received from your bounty through Christ, our Lord, and his Immaculate Mother. Amen.

*   *   *

We thank you, God, for all your gifts and praise you, as all who live must praise you each day; for you teach us in your Scriptures: "When you have eaten your

fill, you shall praise God for the good land
what God has given you." Holy One of
Blessing, we thank you for the land and
its fruit.

—adapted from the Jewish tradition

PSALMS

Psalm 23 [22]

Yahweh is my shepherd,
    I lack nothing.

In meadows of green grass he lets me lie.
To the waters of repose he leads me;
    there he revives my soul.

He guides me by paths of virtue
    for the sake of his name.

Though I pass through a gloomy valley,
    I fear no harm;
beside me your rod and your staff
    are there, to hearten me.

You prepare a table for me
    under the eyes of my enemies;
you anoint my head with oil,
    my cup brims over.

Ah, how goodness and kindness pursue me,
    every day of my life;
my home, the house of Yahweh,
    as long as I live.

Glory be to the Father,
    and to the Son, and to the Holy Spirit,
as it was in the beginning, is now,
    and ever shall be, world without end.
    Amen.

Psalm 51 [50]

(The *Miserere*)

Have mercy on me, O God, in your
    goodness,
in your great tenderness, wipe out my
    faults;
wash me clean of my guilt; purify me from
    my sin.

For I am well aware of my faults,
I have sin constantly in mind,
having sinned against none other than you,
having done what you regard as wrong.

You are just when you pass sentence on me,
blameless when you give judgment.
You know I was born guilty,
a sinner from the moment of conception.

Yet, since you love sincerity of heart,
teach me the secret of wisdom.
Purify me with hyssop until I am clean;
wash me until I am whiter than snow.

Instill some joy and gladness into me,
let the bones you have crushed rejoice
      again;
hide your face from my sins,
wipe out my guilt.

God, create a clean heart in me,
put into me a new and constant spirit,
do not banish me from your presence,
do not deprive me of your holy spirit.

Be my savior again, renew my joy,
keep my spirit steady and willing;
and I shall teach transgressors the way to
      you,
and to you the sinners will return.

Save me from death, God my savior,
and my tongue will acclaim your
      righteousness;
Lord, open my lips,
and my mouth will speak out your praise.

Sacrifice gives you no pleasure,
were I to offer you holocaust, you would
      not have it.
My sacrifice is this broken spirit,

you will not scorn this crushed and broken
    heart.

Show your favor graciously to Zion,
rebuild the walls of Jerusalem.
Then there will be proper sacrifice to
    please you
—holocaust and whole oblation—
and young bulls to be offered on your altar.

Praise the Father almighty,
his Son Jesus Christ, our Lord,
the Spirit who dwells in our hearts,
both now and forever. Amen.

Psalm 117 [116]

Alleluia!

Praise Yahweh, all nations,
    extol him all you peoples!
For his love is strong,
    his faithfulness eternal.

Give praise to the Father almighty,
    to his Son, Jesus Christ, the Lord,
to the Spirit who dwells in our hearts,
    both now and forever. Amen.

Psalm 130 [129]

(The *De profundis*)

From the depths I call to you, Yahweh,
Lord, listen to my cry for help!
Listen compassionately
    to my pleading!

If you never overlooked our sins, Yahweh,
Lord, could anyone survive?
But you do forgive us;
    and for that we revere you.

I wait for Yahweh, my soul waits for him,
    I rely on his promise,
    my soul relies on the Lord
    more than a watchman on the coming
of dawn.

Let Israel rely on Yahweh
    as much as the watchman on the dawn!
For it is with Yahweh that mercy is to be
    found,
and a generous redemption;
    it is he who redeems Israel
    from all their sins.
Glory be to the Father,
    and to the Son, and to the Holy Spirit,
    as it was in the beginning, is now,

and ever shall be, world without end.
Amen.

Psalm 133 [132]

How good, how delightful it is
    for all to live together like brothers;

fine as oil on the head,
    running down the beard,
running down Aaron's beard,
    to the collar of his robes;

copious as a Hermon dew
    falling on the heights of Zion,
where Yahweh confers his blessing,
    everlasting life.

Give praise to the Father almighty,
    to his Son, Jesus Christ, the Lord,
to the Spirit who dwells in our hearts,
    both now and forever. Amen.

Psalm 150

Alleluia!

Praise God in his temple on earth.
Praise him in his temple in heaven,
praise him for his mighty achievements,
praise him for his transcendent greatness!

Praise him with blasts of trumpet,
praise him with lyre and harp,
praise him with drums and dancing,
praise him with strings and reeds,
praise him with clashing cymbals,
praise him with clanging cymbals.
Let everything that breathes praise
    Yahweh!

Alleluia!

EVENING PRAYERS

Let my evening prayer ascend before you,
    O Lord.
And let your loving kindness descend upon
    us.

> O Almighty God, I kneel before you
to thank you with all my heart for all the
favors you have bestowed upon me this
day, for my food and drink, my health
and all the powers of my body and soul. I
thank you for all your inspirations, for
your care and protection, and for all
those other mercies of which I am not
aware. I thank you for them all, heavenly
Father, through Jesus Christ our Lord.
Amen.

Hail, Gladdening Light

Hail, gladdening Light, Light and Glory of the Father immortal, the heavenly, holy, and blessed One, O Jesus Christ. Now that we have reached the setting of the sun, and see the evening light, we sing to God, Father, Son, and Holy Spirit. It is fitting at all times to sing a song of praise in measured melody to you, O Son of God, the Giver of life. Behold the universe sings your glory.

I Am Lying Down Tonight

I am lying down tonight as beseems
in the fellowship of Christ, Son of the
    Virgin of ringlets,
in the fellowship of the gracious Father of
    glory,
in the fellowship of the Spirit of powerful
    aid.

I am lying down tonight with God,
and God tonight will lie down with me,

I will not lie down tonight with sin, nor
    shall
sin nor sin's shadow lie down with me.

I am lying down tonight with the Holy
   Spirit
and the Holy Spirit this night will lie down
   with me,

I will lie down this night with the Three of
   my love,
and the Three of my love will lie down
   with me.

—from the Gaelic tradition

The Canticle of Mary

(The *Magnificat*)

My soul proclaims the greatness of the
   Lord
and my spirit exalts in God, my savior;
because he has looked upon his lowly
   handmaid.
Yes, from this day forward
   all generations will call me blessed,
for the Almighty has done great things for
   me.
Holy is his name,
and his mercy reaches from age to age for
   those who fear him.
He has shown the power of his arm,
he has routed the proud of heart.
He has pulled down princes from their
   thrones

and exalted the lowly.
The hungry he has filled with good things,
    the rich sent empty away.
He has come to the help of Israel his
    servant,
    mindful of his mercy
—according to the promise he made to our
    ancestors—
of his mercy to Abraham and to his
    descendants forever.

—Luke 1:46–55

The Confession of Our Sin

I confess to Almighty God, to the blessed Mary, ever virgin, to blessed Michael the archangel, to blessed Joseph, the spouse of the Virgin, to blessed John the Baptist, to the holy apostles Peter and Paul, to all the saints, and to my brothers and sisters, that I have sinned in thought, word, and deed; through my fault, through my own fault, through my own most grievous fault. Therefore I beseech the blessed Mary, ever virgin, blessed Michael the archangel, blessed Joseph, the spouse of the Virgin, blessed John the Baptist, the holy apostles Peter and Paul, all the saints, and my brothers and sisters, to pray to the Lord, our God, for me.

The Act of Contrition

My God, I am sorry for my sins with all my heart. In choosing to do wrong and failing to do good, I have sinned against you whom I should love above all things. I firmly intend, with your help, to do penance, to sin no more, and to avoid whatever leads me to sin. Amen.

The Canticle of Simeon

(The *Nunc dimittis*)

Now, Master, you can let your servant go in
    peace,
just as you promised;
because my eyes have seen the salvation
which you have prepared for all the nations
    to see,
a light to enlighten the pagans
and the glory of your people Israel.

—Luke 2:29–32

Hail, Holy Queen

(The *Salve, Regina*)

Hail, holy Queen, Mother of Mercy, our life, our sweetness, and our hope. To you do we cry, poor banished children of

Eve. To you do we send up our sighs, mourning and weeping in this vale of tears. Turn, then, O most gracious Advocate, your eyes of mercy toward us. And after this our exile, show unto us the blessed Fruit of your womb, Jesus. O clement, O loving, O sweet Virgin Mary!

2

Prayers of Praise

THE DIVINE PRAISES

Blessed be God.
Blessed be his holy Name.
Blessed be Jesus Christ, true God and true
    man.
Blessed be the Name of Jesus.
Blessed be his most Sacred Heart.
Blessed be his most Precious Blood.
Blessed be Jesus in the most Blessed
    Sacrament of the Altar.
Blessed be the Holy Spirit, the Paraclete.
Blessed be the great Mother of God, Mary
    most holy.
Blessed be her holy and immaculate
    Conception.
Blessed be her glorious Assumption.
Blessed be the name of Mary, Virgin and
    Mother.
Blessed be Saint Joseph, her most chaste
    spouse.

Blessed be God in his angels and in his
  saints.

* * *

Praise to the refuge of all.
Praise to the Most Merciful.
Praise to him who is eternal purity.
Praise to the spotless One.
Praise to the Destroyer of sin.
Praise to the Protector of the just.
Praise to the Remover of ignorance.
Praise to the divine Light.
Praise to the true Light.
Praise to the Light of life.
Praise to the Light of the world.
Praise to the Light of the self.
Praise to the inner Light.

> Eternal Light, shining beyond the heav-
> ens, radiant Sun, illuminating all regions,
> above, below, and across, true Light en-
> lightening every person coming into the
> world, dispel the darkness of our hearts
> and enlighten us with the splendor of
> your glory. Amen.
>
> —adapted from the Indian Liturgy

BLESSED ARE YOU

Blessed are you, Lord, our God, King of the universe, who have created everything for your glory.

Blessed are you, Lord, our God, King of the universe, who have fashioned us.

Blessed are you, Lord, our God, King of the universe, who have fashioned us in your image, in the image of your likeness, and prepared for us a building for eternity. Blessed are you, Lord, who fashioned us.

Bring joy and exaltation to the barren one through the ingathering of her children in gladness. Blessed are you, Lord, who gladdens the Church through her children.

Gladden us as you gladdened your creature in the Garden of Eden to the east. Blessed are you, Lord, who gladdens us.

Blessed are you, Lord, our God, King of the universe, who have created joy and gladness, mirth, glad song, pleasure, delight, love, peace, and companionship. Lord, our God, let there soon be heard in

the cities of the earth and the streets of
your cities the sound of joy and the sound
of gladness, the voice of youths from their
song-filled feasts. Blessed are you, who
gladdens us.

—adapted from the Jewish tradition

THE TE DEUM

To you, O God, be praise!
We acknowledge you as Lord.
In you the whole earth worships its ever-
    living Father.
All the angels cry to you, and heaven and
    all its mighty Powers;
the Cherubim and Seraphim continually
    cry aloud:
Holy, holy, holy are you, Lord God of hosts;
your sovereign glory fills all heaven and
    earth.
The triumphant band of Apostles,
the Prophets, that noble company,
the white-robed throng of Martyrs, all sing
    your praise.
Throughout the world the holy Church
    proclaims you,
the Father of majesty unbounded;
your worshipful, true, and only Son,
and the Holy Spirit who befriends us.
You, Christ, are King of Glory,

you, the Father's everlasting Son.

To set us free you took our flesh, not
     shrinking from the Virgin's womb.

You conquered the pains of death and
     opened heaven to all believers.

You sit at the right Hand of God,
     amid your Father's glory.

We believe that you will come to judge the
     world.

Help us, then, we entreat you; help your
     servants whom you have ransomed with
     your precious blood.

Cause them to be numbered with your
     saints in everlasting glory.

Save your people, Lord, and bless your
     heritage.

And govern them and evermore uphold
     them.

Day by day we bless you

and praise your name forever and ever.

Lord, be pleased to keep us this day from
     all sin.

Have mercy on us, Lord, have mercy.

Lord, let your mercy rest upon us, who put
     all our trust in you.

In you, Lord, is my hope; let me never be
     put to confusion.

3

Prayers to the Holy Trinity

CONSECRATION TO THE BLESSED TRINITY

Eternal Father, prostrate in humble adoration at your feet, we consecrate our whole being to the glory of your Son Jesus, the Word Incarnate. You have established him King of our souls; submit to him our souls, our hearts, our bodies, and may nothing within us move without his order, without his inspiration. Grant that united to him we may be borne to your bosom and consumed in the unity of your Love.

O Jesus, unite us to you, in your life all holy, entirely consecrated to your Father and to souls. Be you our justice, our holiness, our redemption, our all. Sanctify us in truth!

O Holy Spirit, love of the Father and the Son, dwell like a burning furnace of love in the center of our hearts. Bear our thoughts, affections, and actions, like ardent flames, continually heavenward into the bosom of the Father. May our whole life be a *Glory be to the Father and to the Son and to the Holy Spirit.*

O Mary, Mother of Christ, Mother of holy Love, fashion us yourself according to the heart of your Son.

—Dom Columba Marmion

PRAYER OF BLESSED ELIZABETH OF THE TRINITY

O my God, Trinity whom I adore! help me to become utterly forgetful of self, that I may establish myself in you, as changeless and as calm as though my soul were already in eternity. May nothing disturb my peace or draw me forth from you, O my immutable Lord! But may I penetrate more deeply every moment into the depths of your Mystery.

Give peace to my soul; make it your heaven, your cherished dwelling place, your home of rest. Let me never leave you there alone, but keep me there all absorbed in you, in living faith, adoring you and wholly yielded up to your creative action.

O my Christ whom I love! crucified by love! I would fain be the bride of your heart; fain would I cover you with glory, and love you . . . until I die of very love! Yes, I realize my weakness, and beg you to clothe me with yourself, to identify my soul with all the movements of your own. Immerse me in yourself; possess me wholly; substitute yourself for me, that my life may be but a radiance of your own. Enter my soul as Adorer, as Restorer, as Savior!

O eternal Word, Utterance of my God! I long to pass my life listening to you, to become docile that I may learn all from you. Through all darkness, all privations, all helplessness, I crave to keep you ever with me and to dwell beneath your lustrous beams. O my beloved Star! So fascinate me that I cannot wander from your Light!

O *consuming Fire!* Spirit of Love! descend within me and reproduce in me, as it were, an incarnation of the Word, that I may be to him another humanity wherein he renews all his mystery. And you, O Father, bend toward your poor little creature and overshadow her, beholding in her none other than your beloved Son, in whom you have set all your pleasure.

O my Three, my All, my Beatitude, infinite Solitude, Immensity wherein I lose myself! I yield myself to you as your prey. Merge yourself in me, that I may be immerged in you until I depart to contemplate in your light the abyss of your greatness!

PRAYER OF WILLIAM OF SAINT THIERRY

You, God the Father,
    by whom as Creator we live,
you, Wisdom of the Father,
    by whom we have been made anew
    and taught to live wisely,
you, Holy Spirit, whom and in whom we
    love,
    and so live happily, and are to live yet
    more so,
you who are Three in the one Substance,
    the one God,

from whom we are,
by whom we are,
in whom we are,
you, from whom we departed by sinning,
to whom we were made unlike,
but away from whom we have not been
allowed to perish,
you, the Beginning, to whom we are
returning,
the Pattern we are following,
the Grace by which we are reconciled,
you we worship and bless!
To you be glory forever! Amen.

4

❧ ❖ ❧

Prayers to the Father

Father, you have shown me how to walk in your footsteps. You are daily transforming me. My heart is filled with joy as you renew and refresh me. You now call me your beloved just as you called Jesus your beloved Son. You have shown me that I am worthy to be called one of your children. Your love for me surpasses my comprehension. Now you are calling me to come closer to you. You are challenging me to a new level of growth. Give me the desire in my heart to rise up and meet this challenge. This I pray in the name of our Lord Jesus. Amen.

*　　*　　*

At every moment of our existence you are present to us, Father. Help us to

be present to one another so that our
presence may be a strength that heals the
wounds of time and gives hope through
Jesus Christ, our Lord and Brother.
Amen.

*   *   *

Father, I praise you with all these my
brothers, and they give voice to my own
heart and to my own silence. We are all
one silence and a diversity of voices. You
have made us together, you have made
us one and many, you have placed me
here in the midst as witness, as awareness, and as joy. Here I am. In me the
world is present and you are present, and
I am a link in the chain of light and presence. You have made me a kind of center,
but a center that is nowhere. And yet I
am "here," let us say I am "here" under
these trees, not others. If I have any
choice to make, it is to live here and perhaps die here. But in any case it is not the
living or the dying that matters, but
speaking your name with confidence in
the light, in this unvisited place; to speak
your name "Father" just by being here as
"son" in the Spirit and the Light which
you have given, and which are no earthly
light. . . . To be here with the silence of
Sonship in my heart is to be a center in

which all things converge upon you. That is surely enough for the time being. Therefore, Father, I beg you to keep me in this silence so that I may learn from it the word of your peace and the word of your mercy and the word of your gentleness to the world and that through them perhaps your word of peace may make itself heard where it has not been possible for anyone to hear it for a long time.

—Thomas Merton

THE COMPASSIONATE ONE

The compassionate One! May he reign over us forever.

The compassionate One! May he be blessed in heaven and on earth.

The compassionate One! May he be praised throughout all generations,
    may he be glorified through us to the ultimate ends,
    and be honored through us to the inscrutable everlasting.

The compassionate One! May he sustain us in honor.

The compassionate One! May he break the yoke of oppression
    from our necks and guide us erect to our land.

The compassionate One! May he send
abundant blessings.

The compassionate One! May he send us
Elijah the Prophet
—may he be remembered for good—
to proclaim to us good tidings, salvation
and consolation.

The compassionate One! May he bless the
master of this house
and the lady of this house,
me (my wife/husband and family) and
all that is mine,
and all who are here,
them, their house, their family, and all
that is theirs
—just as our forefathers and mothers,
Abraham and Sarah,
Isaac and Rebekah,
Jacob, Rachel and Leah,
were blessed in everything.

So may he bless us all together with a
perfect blessing.

And let us say: Amen!

—from the Jewish tradition

5

Prayers to Jesus

Jesus, the Lord
Jesus, the Son of God
Jesus, the Son of Mary
Jesus, the God-man
Jesus, the True Person
Jesus, the Anointed One
Jesus, the True Teacher
Jesus, the Savior

May God, who became manifest in Jesus Christ, enlighten our minds, strengthen our wills, and fill our hearts with love. May God, the Indweller in our hearts, animate us with his life. And may the grace of our Lord Jesus Christ and the love of God and the fellowship of the Holy Spirit be with us all. Amen.

—adapted from an Indian Catholic Liturgy

PRAYER OF SELF-DEDICATION TO JESUS

Lord Jesus Christ, take all my freedom, my memory, my understanding, and my will. All that I have and cherish you have given to me. I surrender it all to be guided by your will. Your grace and your love are wealth enough for me. Give me these, Lord Jesus; I ask for nothing more.

O JESUS LIVING IN MARY

O Jesus living in Mary,
come and live in your servants,
in the spirit of your holiness,
in the fullness of your might,
in the truth of your virtues,
in the perfection of your ways,
in the communion of your mysteries,
in your Spirit, for the glory of your Father.
  Amen.

HEART OF JESUS

Heart of Jesus in my heart,
  my heart in thee,

unto thy Father's love in unity of love
    offer me.

Light of Jesus, illumine me
    to see whatever woundeth thee;
that I may sin not unto thee,
    cleanse me.

Power of Jesus in every part,
    from sin heal me;
that nothing be except thy love,
    inflame me.

—Gilbert Shaw

PRAYER IN HONOR OF THE SACRED HEART

O God, you most mercifully granted to bestow on us in the Heart of your Son, wounded for our sins, an infinite source of love. Grant that we, who render to him the homage of our affection, may also make worthy reparation for our sins. We ask this through Christ, our Lord.

PRAYER FROM THE BYZANTINE TRADITION

Sovereign of heaven, King of the earth, Master, too, of the world below,

Christ, the Apostles paid court to you on earth while Elijah came from heaven and Moses from the dead to join in singing your praises. Lord Christ, let all peoples extol you. You converted me by your divine Love. Burn away my sins in the spiritual flame, that I, too, may joyfully behold you. Amen.

PRAYER TO JESUS CHRIST THE KING

O Christ Jesus, I acknowledge you to be the King of the universe. All that has been made is created for you. Exercise over me all your sovereign rights. I renew the promises of my baptism, renouncing Satan and all of his works and pomps, and I engage myself to live a truly Christian life. In a special way, I engage myself to seek the triumph of your dominion over us all. Divine Lord, I offer you my poor actions to help obtain the acknowledgment by every heart of your sacred kingly rule. May the kingdom of your peace be established throughout all the earth. Amen.

PRAYER IN HONOR OF THE BLESSED SACRAMENT

O God, under this wonderful Sacrament, you have left us a memorial of your Passion. Grant, we ask, that we may so venerate the mysteries of your Body and Blood that we may ever experience within ourselves the fruit of your redemption, you who live and reign with the Father and the Holy Spirit, forever and ever. Amen.

6

❧ ❖ ❧

Prayers to
the Holy Spirit

MORNING PRAYER

Jesus, you have sent me your Spirit. Make me constantly aware of his presence in my daily life. May the power of his love help me forgive all who have hurt me and make us one again.

May every hurt I have caused others be healed by the power of your Holy Spirit's loving presence within me. Protect me from damaging any relationships today and heal any damaged relationships already present.

Holy Spirit, if there is anything I should do to heal wounds which I have inflicted, give me grace to do it lovingly today.

Fill me with your presence,
Holy Spirit, now and forever.

Thank you for doing this today.
Amen.

COME, HOLY SPIRIT

Come, Holy Spirit, fill the hearts of your
   faithful
and kindle in them the fire of your love.

Send forth your Spirit and they shall be
   created,
and you will renew the face of the earth.

Let us pray.

O God, on the first Pentecost you instructed
those who believed in you by the light of the
Holy Spirit; under the inspiration of the same
Spirit, give us a taste for what is right and true
and a continuing sense of his presence and
power, through Jesus Christ, our Lord. Amen.

COME, HOLY SPIRIT:

The Sequence, Veni, Sancte Spiritus

Come, Holy Spirit, come!
And from your celestial home
shed a ray of light divine.

Come, Father of the poor!
Come, Source of all our store!
Come, within our bosoms shine!

You, of comforters the best;
you, the soul's most welcome Guest;
sweet refreshment here below;

In our labor, rest most sweet;
grateful coolness in the heat;
solace in the midst of woe.

O most blessed Light divine,
shine within these hearts of thine,
and our inmost being fill!

Where you are not, man has naught,
nothing good in deed or thought,
nothing free from taint of ill.

Heal our wounds, our strength renew;
on our dryness, pour your dew;
wash the stains of guilt away.

Bend the stubborn heart and will;
melt the frozen, warm the chill;
guide the steps that go astray.

On the faithful, who adore
and confess you, evermore
in your sev'nfold gift descend.

Give them virtue's sure reward;
give them your salvation, Lord;
give them joys that never end. Amen.
    Alleluia.

PRAYER OF WILLIAM OF SAINT THIERRY TO THE HOLY SPIRIT

O Love, O Fire, O Charity, come into us! Be you our leader and our light, the fire that consumes and burns in the repentant sinner, be you our paraclete, our comforter, our advocate and helper in all the things for which we pray. Show us what we believe. Grant that for which we hope. And make our faces like unto the face of God. Amen.

7

Prayers to the Blessed Virgin Mary

THE MEMORARE

Remember, O most gracious Virgin Mary, that never was it known that anyone who fled to your protection, implored your help, or sought your intercession was left unaided. Inspired with this confidence, I fly unto you, O Virgin of virgins, my Mother. To you I come, before you I stand, sinful and sorrowful. O Mother of the Word Incarnate, despise not my petitions, but in your mercy hear and answer me.

—Saint Bernard of Clairvaux

WE PLACE OURSELVES IN YOUR KEEPING

(The Sub tuum)

We place ourselves in your keeping, holy Mother of God. Refuse not the prayer of your children in their distress, but deliver us from all danger, ever virgin, glorious and blessed.

AT THE CROSS

(The Stabat Mater)

At the Cross her station keeping,
stood the mournful Mother weeping,
while her Jesus hung above.

Through her heart his sorrow sharing,
all his bitter anguish bearing,
ran the sword of suffering love.

Mournful Mother, let me borrow,
some of that most bitter sorrow,
which for Jesus you did feel.

That my heart, new fervor gaining,
more devoted love attaining,
may to his pierced heart appeal.

By the cross of my salvation,
one with you in reparation,
may he all my sins forgive.

Be his wounds my consolation,
be his passion my salvation,
be his dying my belief.

Christ, my Lord, in my last hour,
grant that through your Mother's power
I may conquer every sin.

When my soul and body sever,
may I live with you forever,
to your glory ent'ring in. Amen.

ACT OF CONSECRATION TO THE IMMACULATE HEART OF MARY

O most holy Virgin Mary, Mother of God, I, although most unworthy of being your servant, yet moved by your wonderful mercy and by the desire to serve you, consecrate myself to your Immaculate Heart, and choose you today, in the presence of my Guardian Angel and the whole heavenly court, for my special Lady, Advocate, and Mother. I firmly resolve that I will love and serve you always, and do whatever I can to lead others to love and serve you. I pray, Mother of God, and my most kind and amiable Mother, that you will receive me into the number of your servants as your servant and child forever. Purify more all my thoughts, words, and actions at every moment of my life, that every step and breath may be directed to the greater glory of God, and through your most powerful intercession obtain for me that I may never more offend my beloved Jesus, that I may glorify him in you, in the company of the Blessed Trinity, through eternity in Paradise.

ACT OF CONSECRATION OF SAINT LOUIS MARIE DE MONTFORT

In the presence of all the heavenly court I choose you this day for my Mother and Mistress. I deliver and consecrate to you, as your slave, my body and soul, my goods, both interior and exterior, and even the value of all my good actions, past, present, and future; leaving to you the entire and full right of disposing of me, and all that belongs to me, without exception, according to your good pleasure, for the greater glory of God, in time and eternity. Amen.

CONSECRATION OF THE WORLD TO MARY

Hail to you, Mary, who are wholly united to the redeeming consecration of your Son!

Mother of the Church, enlighten the people of God along the paths of faith, hope, and love. Help us to live in the truth of the consecration of Christ for the entire human family of the modern world.

In entrusting to you, O Mother, the world, all individuals and people, we also entrust to you this very consecration of the world, placing it in your motherly heart.

Immaculate Heart of Mary, help us to conquer the menace of evil, which so easily takes root in the hearts of the people today, and whose immeasurable effects already weigh down upon our modern world and seem to block the path toward the future.

From famine and war, *deliver us.*
From nuclear war, from incalculable self-
   destruction, from every kind of war,

From sins against human life from its very
    beginning,
From hatred and from demeaning the
    dignity of the children of God,
From every kind of injustice in the life of
    society, both national and international,
From readiness to trample on the
    commandments of God,
From attempts to stifle in human hearts the
    very truth of God,
From the loss of awareness of good and
    evil,
From sins against the Holy Spirit.

Accept, O Mother, this cry with the sufferings of all individual human beings, laden with the sufferings of whole societies.

Help us, with the power of the Holy Spirit, to conquer all sin: individual sin and the "sin of the world," sin in all its manifestations. Let there be revealed once more in the history of the world the infinite saving power of the redemption: the power of merciful love. May it put a stop to evil. May it transform consciences. May your Immaculate Heart reveal for all the light of hope.

—Pope John Paul II

ACT OF REPARATION

For the First Saturday of the Month

O most holy Virgin and our Mother, we listen with grief to the complaints of your Immaculate Heart surrounded with thorns which we ungrateful ones place therein at every moment by our infidelity and ingratitude. Moved by the ardent desire of loving you as our Mother and of promoting a true devotion to your Immaculate Heart we prostrate ourselves at your feet to prove the sorrow we feel for the grievances that we cause you, and to atone, by means of our prayers and sacrifices with which we return your tender love.

Obtain for us the pardon of our many sins. A word from you will obtain grace and amendment for us all. Hasten, O Lady, the conversion of us sinners, that we may love Jesus and cease to offend the Lord, already so much offended, and escape the pains of hell.

Turn your eyes of mercy toward us, that henceforth we may love God with all

our hearts while on earth and enjoy him
forever in heaven. Amen.

SOUL OF MARY

Soul of Mary, sanctify me.
Heart of Mary, inflame me.
Hands of Mary, support me.
Feet of Mary, direct me.
Immaculate eyes of Mary, look upon me.
Lips of Mary, speak for me.
O Mary, hear me.
In the wound of the Heart of Jesus, hide
   me.
Let me never be separated from thee.
From my enemy defend me.
At the hour of my death call me.
And bid me come to your Immaculate
   Heart;
that thus I may come to the Heart of Jesus
and there with the saints praise thee
for all eternity. Amen.

O MOST CHASTE VIRGIN MARY

O most chaste Virgin Mary, I beseech you by that unspotted purity
wherewith you did prepare for the Son of
God a dwelling of delight in your virginal

womb, that by your intercession I may be cleansed from every stain of sin.

O most humble Virgin Mary, I beseech you by that most profound humility whereby you did merit to be raised above all the choirs of the angels and the saints, that, by your intercession, all my negligences may be expiated.

O most loving Virgin Mary, I beseech you, by that ineffable love which united you so closely and so inseparably to God, that, by your intercession, I may obtain an abundance of all merits. Amen.

—taught to Saint Gertrude by Mary

PRAYER OF OUR LADY OF MOUNT CARMEL

O God, you have honored the Order of Carmel with the special title of your Blessed Mother Mary, ever Virgin. Grant in your mercy that we who keep her memory this day may be shielded by her protection and be found worthy to attain eternal joy. You who live and reign with the Son and the Holy Spirit, God, now and forever. Amen.

PRAYER TO OUR LADY
OF WALSINGHAM

O alone of all women, mother and virgin, Mother most happy, Virgin most pure, now we, sinful as we are, come to you who are all pure. We salute you. We honor you, as we may, with our humble offerings. May your Son grant us, that imitating you, we also, by the grace of the Holy Spirit, may deserve spiritually to conceive the Lord Jesus in our inmost soul, and once conceived, never to lose him. Amen.

PRAYER TO MARY FOR THE SICK

Mary, Health of the Sick,
be at the bedside of all the world's sick;
of those who are unconscious and dying;
of those who have begun their agony;
of those who have abandoned all hope of a
    cure;
of those who weep and cry out in pain;
of those who cannot receive care
    because they have no money;
of those who ought to be resting
    but are forced by poverty to work;

of those who pass long nights
    sleeplessly;
of those who seek vainly in their beds
    for a less painful position;
of those who are tormented by the
    cares
    of a family in distress;
of those who must renounce
    their most cherished plans for the
    future;
of those, above all, who do not believe
    in a better life;
of those who rebel and curse God;
of those who do not know that
    Christ suffered
    like them and for them.

Amen.

FROM THE BYZANTINE LITURGY

It is fitting and right to call you blessed, O Mother of God; you are ever blessed and all-blameless and the Mother of our God. Higher in honor than the Cherubim and more glorious without compare than the Seraphim, you gave birth to God the Word in virginity. You are truly Mother of God; you do we magnify.

—from the Liturgy of Saint John Chrysostom

In you, Woman full of grace, all creation exalts, the hierarchy of angels together with the human race. In you, sanctified Temple, spiritual Paradise, Glory of virgins of whom God took flesh—from whom our God who exists before the world became a child. For he has made your womb his throne, making it more spacious than the heavens. In you, O Woman full of grace, all creation exalts. Glory to you!

—from the Liturgy of Saint Basil

8

Litanies

LITANY OF THE HOLY NAME OF JESUS

Lord, have mercy.
Christ, have mercy.
Lord, have mercy.
Christ, hear us.
Christ, graciously hear us.
God, the Father of heaven, have mercy on us.
God the Son, Redeemer of the world, have mercy on us.
God the Holy Spirit, have mercy on us.
Holy Trinity, one God, have mercy on us.
Jesus, Son of the living God, *have mercy on us.*
Jesus, splendor of the Father,
Jesus, Brightness of eternal Light,
Jesus, King of Glory,
Jesus, Son of Justice,
Jesus, Son of the Virgin Mary,

Jesus, most amiable,
Jesus, most admirable,
Jesus, the mighty God,
Jesus, Father of the world to come,
Jesus, most powerful,
Jesus, most patient,
Jesus, most obedient,
Jesus, meek and humble of heart,
Jesus, Lover of chastity,
Jesus, our Lover,
Jesus, God of Peace,
Jesus, Author of life,
Jesus, Model of virtues,
Jesus, zealous for souls,
Jesus, our God,
Jesus, our Refuge,
Jesus, Father of the poor,
Jesus, Treasure of the faithful,
Jesus, good Shepherd,
Jesus, true Light,
Jesus, eternal Wisdom,
Jesus, infinite Goodness,
Jesus, our Way and our Life,
Jesus, joy of angels,
Jesus, King of the Patriarchs,
Jesus, Master of the Apostles,
Jesus, Teacher of the Evangelists,
Jesus, strength of martyrs,
Jesus, light of confessors,
Jesus, purity of virgins,
Jesus, crown of all saints,

Be merciful, spare us, O Jesus.
Be merciful, graciously hear us, O Jesus.
From all evil, *deliver us, O Jesus.*
From all sin,
From your wrath,
From the snares of the devil,
From the spirit of fornication,
From everlasting death,
From the neglect of your inspirations,
Through the mystery of your incarnation,
Through your nativity,
Through your infancy,
Through your most holy life,
Through your agony and passion,
Through your Cross and dereliction,
Through your sufferings,
Through your death and burial,
Through your resurrection,
Through your ascension,
Through your institution of the Holy
    Eucharist,
Through your joys,
Through your glory,
Lamb of God, who take away the sins of
    the world, spare us, O Jesus.
Lamb of God, who take away the sins of
    the world, hear us, O Jesus.
Lamb of God, who take away the sins of
    the world, have mercy on us, O Jesus.
Jesus, hear us.
Jesus, graciously hear us.

Let us pray.

O Lord Jesus Christ, who has said, "Ask and you shall receive; seek and you shall find; knock and it shall be opened unto you"; mercifully attend to our supplications, and grant us the grace of your divine love, that we may love you with all our hearts, and in all our words and actions, and never cease to praise you. Make us, O Lord, to have a perpetual fear and love of your Name, for you never fail to govern those whom you solidly establish in your love, you who live and reign forever and ever. Amen.

LITANY OF THE SACRED HEART OF JESUS

Lord, have mercy.

Christ, have mercy.

Lord, have mercy.

Christ, hear us.

Christ, graciously hear us.

God, the Father of heaven, have mercy on us.

God the Son, Redeemer of the world, have mercy on us.

God the Holy Spirit, have mercy on us.

Holy Trinity, one God, have mercy on us.

Heart of Jesus, Son of the eternal Father,
have mercy on us.

Heart of Jesus, formed by the Holy Spirit
in the womb of the Virgin Mother,

Heart of Jesus, substantially united to the
Word of God,

Heart of Jesus, of infinite majesty,

Heart of Jesus, Temple of God,

Heart of Jesus, Tabernacle of the Most
High,

Heart of Jesus, House of God and Gate of
heaven,

Heart of Jesus, burning furnace of charity,

Heart of Jesus, abode of justice and love,

Heart of Jesus, abyss of all virtue,

Heart of Jesus, most worthy of all praise,

Heart of Jesus, King and center of all
hearts,

Heart of Jesus, in whom are all the
resources of wisdom and knowledge,

Heart of Jesus, in whom dwells the fullness
of the divinity,

Heart of Jesus, in whom the Father is well
pleased,

Heart of Jesus, of whose fullness we have
all received,

Heart of Jesus, desire of the everlasting
hills,

Heart of Jesus, patient and most merciful,

Heart of Jesus, enriching all who evoke
you,

Heart of Jesus, fountain of life and holiness,

Heart of Jesus, propitiation for our sins,

Heart of Jesus, loaded down with opprobrium,

Heart of Jesus, obedient unto death,

Heart of Jesus, pierced with a lance,

Heart of Jesus, source of all consolation,

Heart of Jesus, our life and resurrection,

Heart of Jesus, our peace and reconciliation,

Heart of Jesus, victim for our sins,

Heart of Jesus, salvation of those who trust in you,

Heart of Jesus, hope of those who die in you,

Heart of Jesus, delight of all the saints,

Lamb of God, who take away the sins of the world, spare us, O Lord.

Lamb of God, who take away the sins of the world, hear us, O Lord.

Lamb of God, who take away the sins of the world, have mercy on us, O Lord.

Jesus, meek and humble of heart;

Make our hearts like unto thine.

Let us pray.

Almighty and eternal God, look upon the heart of your most beloved Son and upon the praises and satisfaction he offers you in the name of sinners; and to those who implore your mercy in your great goodness grant forgiveness in the name of Jesus Christ, your Son, who lives and reigns forever and ever. Amen.

LITANY OF THE BLESSED VIRGIN MARY

Lord, have mercy.
Christ, have mercy.
Lord, have mercy.
Christ, hear us.
Christ, graciously hear us.
God, the Father of heaven, have mercy on us.
God the Son, Redeemer of the world, have mercy on us.
God the Holy Spirit, have mercy on us.
Holy Trinity, one God, have mercy on us.
Holy Mary, *pray for us*.
Holy Mother of God,
Holy Virgin of virgins,
Mother of Christ,
Mother most pure,
Mother most chaste,
Mother inviolate,
Mother undefiled,
Mother most amiable,
Mother most admirable,
Mother of good counsel,
Mother of our Creator,

Mother of our savior,
Virgin most prudent,
Virgin most venerable,
Virgin most renowned,
Virgin most powerful,
Virgin most merciful,
Virgin most faithful,
Mirror of justice,
Seat of wisdom,
Cause of our joy,
Spiritual vessel,
Vessel of honor,
Singular vessel of devotion,
Mystical Rose,
Tower of David,
Tower of Ivory,
House of Gold,
Ark of the Covenant,
Gate of Heaven,
Morning Star,
Health of the sick,
Refuge of sinners,
Comforter of the afflicted,
Help of Christians,
Queen of angels,
Queen of patriarchs,
Queen of prophets,
Queen of apostles,
Queen of martyrs,
Queen of confessors,
Queen of virgins,

Queen of all saints,
Queen conceived without original sin,
Queen assumed into heaven,
Queen of the most holy Rosary,
Queen of Peace,
Lamb of God, who take away the sins of
    the world, spare us, O Lord.
Lamb of God, who take away the sins of
    the world, hear us, O Lord.
Lamb of God, who take away the sins of
    the world, have mercy on us, O Lord.
Pray for us, O holy Mother of God,
That we may be made worthy of the
    promises of Christ.

Let us pray.

> Grant we beseech you, O Lord God, that
> we, your servants, may enjoy lasting
> health of mind and body, and by the glo-
> rious intercession of the Blessed Mary,
> ever virgin, be delivered from present
> sorrow and enter into the joy of eternal
> happiness. Through Christ, our Lord.
> Amen.

LITANY OF SAINT JOSEPH

Lord, have mercy.
Christ, have mercy.

Lord, have mercy.
Christ, hear us.
Christ, graciously hear us.
God, the Father of heaven, have mercy on
    us.
God the Son, Redeemer of the world, have
    mercy on us.
God the Holy Spirit, have mercy on us.
Holy Trinity, one God, have mercy on us.
Holy Mary, *pray for us.*
Saint Joseph,
Renowned offspring of David,
Light of Patriarchs,
Spouse of the Mother of God,
Chaste Guardian of the Virgin,
Foster Father of the Son of God,
Diligent Protector of Christ,
Head of the Holy Family,
Joseph most just,
Joseph most chaste,
Joseph most prudent,
Joseph most obedient,
Joseph most strong,
Joseph most faithful,
Mirror of patience,
Lover of poverty,
Model of artisans,
Glory of home life,
Guardian of virgins,
Pillar of families,
Solace of the wretched,

Hope of the sick,
Patron of the dying,
Terror of demons,
Protector of the Church,
Lamb of God, who take away the sins of
the world, spare us, O Lord.
Lamb of God, who take away the sins of
the world, hear us, O Lord.
Lamb of God, who take away the sins of
the world, have mercy on us, O Lord.
He made him the lord of his household,
And prince over all his possessions.

Let us pray.

O God, who in your ineffable providence
did vouchsafe to choose blessed Joseph
spouse of your most holy Mother, grant
we beseech you that we may be worthy
to have him for our intercessor in heaven
whom we venerate on earth as our protector. Amen.

LITANY OF THE SAINTS

Lord, have mercy.
Christ, have mercy.
Lord, have mercy.
Christ, hear us.
Christ, graciously hear us.

God, the Father of heaven, have mercy on us.

God the Son, Redeemer of the world, have mercy on us.

God the Holy Spirit, have mercy on us.

Holy Trinity, one God, have mercy on us.

Holy Mary, *pray for us.*

Holy Mother of God,

Holy Virgin of virgins,

Saint Michael,

Saint Gabriel,

Saint Raphael,

All you holy angels and archangels,

All you holy orders of blessed spirits,

Saint John the Baptist,

Saint Joseph,

All you holy patriarchs and prophets,

Saint Peter,

Saint Paul,

Saint Andrew,

Saint John,

All you holy apostles and evangelists,

All you holy disciples of the Lord,

Saint Stephen,

Saint Lawrence,

Saint Vincent,

All you holy martyrs,

Saint Sylvester,

Saint Gregory,

Saint Augustine,

All you holy bishops and confessors,
All you holy doctors,
Saint Anthony,
Saint Benedict,
Saint Dominic,
Saint Francis,
All you holy priests and Levites,
All you holy monks and hermits,
Saint Mary Magdalene,
Saint Agnes,
Saint Cecilia,
Saint Agatha,
Saint Anastasia,
All you holy men and women, saints of
    God, make intercession for us.
Be merciful to us; spare us, O Lord.
Be merciful to us; graciously hear us, O
    Lord.
From all evil, *O Lord, deliver us.*
From all sin,
Through the mystery of your holy
    Incarnation,
Through your coming,
Through your Nativity,
Through your Baptism and fasting,
Through your Cross and Passion,
Through your Death and Burial,
Through your Resurrection,
Through your Ascension,

Through the coming of the Holy Spirit, the
    comforter,
In the day of judgment,
We sinners, *we beseech you, hear us.*
That you might spare us,
That you vouchsafe to rule and preserve
    your holy Church,
That you vouchsafe to preserve our Holy
    Father and all the bishops,
That you vouchsafe to humble the enemies
    of your holy Church,
That you vouchsafe to grant peace and true
    concord to all nations,
That you vouchsafe to confirm and
    preserve us in your holy service,
That you vouchsafe to render eternal
    blessings to all our benefactors,
That you vouchsafe to give and preserve
    the fruits of the earth,
That you vouchsafe to give eternal rest to
    all the faithful departed,
That you would vouchsafe graciously to
    hear us,
Lamb of God, who take away the sins of
    the world, spare us, O Lord.
Lamb of God, who take away the sins of
    the world, hear us, O Lord.
Lamb of God, who take away the sins of
    the world, have mercy on us, O Lord.
Christ, hear us.
Christ, graciously hear us.

Let us pray.

Almighty and everlasting God, you have dominion over the living and the dead and have mercy on all those who serve you faithfully with good works. We humbly ask that those for whom we pray, whether still present in this world or already in the world to come, may, through the intercession of your saints, by the clemency of your goodness, obtain the remission of all their sins and life everlasting, through Christ, our Lord. Amen.

THE LITANY OF PEACE

In peace let us pray to the Lord. Lord, have mercy.

For the peace from on high and for the salvation of our souls, let us pray to the Lord. *Lord, have mercy.*

For peace in the whole world, the well-being of the holy Churches of God, and the union of all, let us pray to the Lord. *Lord, have mercy.*

For this holy place, and for those who enter it with faith, reverence, and the fear of God, let us pray to the Lord. *Lord, have mercy.*

For his Holiness, John Paul of Rome, our most reverend bishop, N., the priests, the deacons in Christ, and for all the clergy and people, let us pray to the Lord. *Lord, have mercy.*

For our public servants, for the government, and for all who protect us, that they may be strengthened and upheld in every good deed, let us pray to the Lord. *Lord, have mercy.*

For this place, for every city and country place and the faithful dwelling in them, let us pray to the Lord. *Lord, have mercy.*

For favorable weather, the abundance of the fruits of the earth, and for peaceful times, let us pray to the Lord. *Lord, have mercy.*

For the travelers by sea, air, and land, for the sick, the suffering, for those in prison, and their salvation, let us pray to the Lord. *Lord, have mercy.*

For our deliverance from all affliction, wrath, danger, and need, let us pray to the Lord. *Lord, have mercy.*

Help us, save us, have mercy on us, and protect us, O God, by your grace. *Lord, have mercy.*

Let us remember our all-holy, spotless, most highly blessed, and glorious Lady, the Mother of God and ever virgin Mary, with all the saints, and commend ourselves and one another and our whole life to Christ God. *To you, O Lord.*

Lord our God, whose power is without compare, whose glory is incomprehensible, whose mercy is beyond measure and whose love for mankind is beyond word, be pleased, Master, in the depth of your compassion, to look down on us and this holy place, and make us and those praying with us obtain the riches of your mercies and your tender pity. For all glory, honor, and worship are your due, Father, Son, and Holy Spirit, now and always and forever and ever. Amen.

9

Prayers to the Saints

PRAYER TO SAINT JOSEPH

Holy father Joseph, to whose faithful custody Christ Jesus and Mary the Virgin Mother were committed, I beg you, by your dear pledges, Jesus and Mary, that, being preserved from all uncleanness, I may with spotless mind, pure heart, and chaste body ever serve Jesus and Mary most chastely all the days of my life. Amen.

PRAYER TO SAINT ANNE

O good Saint Anne, Mother of the Mother of God, I come to you with confidence. Jesus could not but heed his Mother and she will always listen to you. I entrust myself to you in body and in spirit. Help me be faithful to the interior life and the spirit of prayer. Help me to use the things of this world in a way that is good for me and for all my sisters and brothers, who have been redeemed by the life of your Grandson. O Grandmother of God, and my Grandmother, take care of me and bring me safely to my heavenly home. Amen.

PRAYER TO SAINT JOHN

Beloved disciple of the Lord, faithful priest, teacher of the Word of God, help us to hunger for the Word, to be loyal to the Master, and to love one another.

PRAYER TO SAINTS PETER AND PAUL

O holy apostles, Peter and Paul, I choose you this day and forever to be my special patrons and advocates; you, Saint Peter, Prince of the Apostles, because you are the Rock, upon which Almighty God has built his Church; you, Saint Paul, because you were chosen by God as the vessel of election and the preacher of truth in the whole world. Obtain for us, I pray you, lively faith, firm hope, and burning love; complete detachment from ourselves, contempt for worldliness, patience in adversity, humility in prosperity, attention in prayer, purity of heart, a right intention in all our works, diligence in fulfilling the duties of our state in life, constancy in our resolutions, resignation to the will of God, and perseverance in the grace of God even unto death; so that, by means of your intercession and your glorious merits, we may be able to overcome the temptations of the world, the flesh, and the devil, and may be made worthy to appear before the chief and eternal Shepherd, Jesus Christ, who with the Father and the Holy Spirit lives and reigns for endless ages, to enjoy his presence and love him forever. Amen.

PRAYER TO SAINT JUDE

O glorious Saint Jude, by those sublime prerogatives wherewith you were ennobled in your lifetime, your kinship with our Lord Jesus Christ according to the flesh and your vocation to be an apostle, by that glory which now is yours in heaven as the reward of your apostolic labors and your martyrdom, obtain for us from the Giver of every good and perfect gift all the graces whereof we stand in need in order to treasure up in our hearts the divinely inspired doctrines which you have transmitted to us in your Epistle: to build our edifice of perfection upon our most holy faith, praying by the grace of the Holy Spirit to keep ourselves in the love of God, looking for the mercy of Jesus Christ unto eternal life; to strive by all means to help those who go astray; exalting thus the glory and majesty, the dominion and power of him who is able to keep us without sin and to present us spotless with exceeding joy at the coming of our Divine Savior, the Lord Jesus Christ. Amen.

PRAYER TO SAINT MICHAEL, THE ARCHANGEL

Saint Michael, Archangel, defend us in battle, be our protection against the wickedness and snares of the devil; may God rebuke him, we humbly pray; and do you, O Prince of the heavenly host, by the power of God, thrust into hell Satan and all evil spirits, who wander through the world for the ruin of souls. Amen.

PRAYER TO SAINT FRANCIS OF ASSISI

O blessed Saint Francis, lover of Lady Poverty, teach us to love her, too. In these our days when so many of our brothers and sisters suffer so much from the lack of the basic necessities of life, help us who are better off to learn how to share what we have even to the point of depriving ourselves. Raise up in the world leaders who will know how to reshape the economy so that no one will want at the abundant table of the Lord, each content with the wonderful portion the Lord has allotted, just as you found great joy in the common heritage of the human family. O holy Poor Man of Assisi, pray for us, now and at the hour of our death. Amen.

PRAYER TO SAINT THOMAS À BECKET

Saint Thomas, by your life you showed us that wealth, power, and prestige are nothing compared to following

Christ. Pray for us, who are encompassed by the temptations of the commercial world, that we may turn away from it, and turn toward the example of our savior, Jesus, as you have done.

Pray that we may also stand firm in our faith and in our love for Christ and our fellows as you did when the evil soldiers sank their swords into your flesh at the altar of Christ.

PRAYER TO SAINT FRANCIS XAVIER

O most lovable and loving Saint Francis Xavier, in union with you I adore the Divine Majesty. The remembrance of the favors with which God blessed you during life and your glory after death fills me with joy, and I unite with you in offering to him my humble tribute of thanksgiving and of praise. I implore you to secure for me, through your most powerful intercession, the inestimable blessing of living and dying in the state of grace. I also beseech you to obtain the other particular favors I seek. But if what I ask is not for the glory of God and for the good of my soul, please obtain for me what is most conducive to both. Amen.

PRAYER TO SAINT ANTHONY OF PADUA

O wondrous Saint Anthony, glorious by reason of the fame of your miracles, you had the happiness of receiving into your arms our Blessed Lord as a little child. Obtain for us from his bounty the favors we seek. You were so gracious to poor sinners, regard not our lack of merit but consider the glory of God, which will be exalted once more through you in the salvation of our souls.

As a pledge of our gratitude, I ask you to accept my promise to live more according to the teachings of the Gospel and to be devoted in the service of the poor whom you have ever loved in a special way. Bless my resolution and obtain for me the grace to be faithful to it until death. Amen.

PRAYER TO SAINT THÉRÈSE, THE LITTLE FLOWER

The Lord said, "Unless you be converted, and become as little children, you shall not enter into the Kingdom of Heaven." Obtain for us, we beseech you, so to follow in your footsteps with humility and simplicity of heart that we may obtain the everlasting reward. Amen.

PRAYER TO SAINT MAXIMILIAN KOLBE

The Lord Jesus Christ said, "Greater love than this no man has than that he lay down his life for his friends." Through your intercession, Saint Maximilian, whose life illustrated such love, we ask for a deep and sincere love for all our fellow humans.

Through your Knights of the Immaculate, you spread a fervent devotion to our Lady. You gave up your life for a total stranger and loved your persecutors, giving us an example of unselfish love of all —a love which was inspired by true devotion to Mary. Obtain for us from the Lord

Jesus Christ that we too may give ourselves entirely without reserve to the love and service of our heavenly Queen in order to better love and serve our fellows.

Pray for us, O Immaculate Mother.

Pray for us, Saint Maximilian.

PRAYER TO MY PATRON SAINT

O heavenly Patron, in whose name I glory, pray ever to God for me that he may strengthen me in my faith, establish me in virtue, and guard me in conflict, so that I might overcome all evil and attain to everlasting glory with you. Amen.

10

Prayers of
the Friends of God

PRAYER OF SAINT AUGUSTINE

Breathe in me, Holy Spirit, that all my thoughts may be holy. Act in me, Holy Spirit, that my work may also be holy. Draw my heart, Holy Spirit, that I may love only what is holy. Strengthen me, Holy Spirit, to defend all that is holy. Guard me, Holy Spirit, that I may always be holy.

PRAYER OF SAINT PATRICK

Christ, as a light, illumine and guide me!
Christ, as a shield, overshadow and cover me!
Christ, be under me!
Christ, be over me!

Christ, be beside me
   on left hand and right!
Christ, this day be within and without me!
Christ, the lowly and meek,
Christ, the all powerful,
   be in the heart of each one to whom I
     speak—
   in the mouth of each one who speaks to
     me—
   in all who draw near to me, or see me,
     or hear me.

                            Amen.

PRAYER OF SAINT BEDE

O Lord, Almighty God, open wide my heart and teach it by the grace of your Holy Spirit to ask for what is pleasing to you. Direct my thoughts and senses so to think and to act that, by a worthy manner of life, I may deserve to obtain the eternal joys of the heavenly kingdom. Direct my actions according to your commands so that, ever striving to keep them in my life, I may receive for my deeds the eternal reward. Amen.

PRAYER OF SAINT BERNARD OF CLAIRVAUX

Jesus, hope of the penitent,
>   how kind you are to those who ask,
>   how good you are to those who seek.
What must you be to those who find?

PRAYER OF WILLIAM OF SAINT THIERRY

> Have mercy on us, Lord, have mercy on us! You are our Potter and we are the clay. Somehow or other we have held together until now; we are still carried by your mighty hand, and we are still clinging to your three fingers, faith, hope, and charity, with which you support the whole great bulk of each—that is to say, the whole weight of your holy Church. Cleanse our reins and our hearts by the fire of your Holy Spirit, and establish the work that you have wrought in us, lest we be loosed asunder and return again to clay or nothingness. We were created for you by yourself, and toward you our face is set. We acknowledge you our Maker and Creator; we adore your wisdom and

pray that it may order all our life. We
adore your goodness and mercy, and beg
them ever to sustain and help us. You
who have made us, bring us to perfection; perfect in us the image and likeness
of yourself for which you made us. Amen.

PRAYER OF SAINT AELRED

(From his *Pastoral Prayer*)

Lord, look at my soul's wounds,
your living and effective eye sees
everything.
It pierces like a sword, even to part
asunder soul and spirit.
Assuredly, my Lord, you see in my soul
the traces of my former sins,
my present perils,
and also motives and occasions for
others yet to be.
You see those things, Lord,
and I would have you see them.
You know well, O Searcher of my heart,
that there is nothing in my soul
that I would hide from you,
even had I the power to escape your eyes.
Woe to the souls that want to hide
themselves from you.
They cannot make themselves not

to be seen by you,
but only miss your healing
and incur your punishment.
So see me, sweet Lord, see me.
My hope, most merciful, is in your loving
kindness;
for you will see me,
either as a good physician sees,
intent upon my healing,
or else as a kind master, anxious to correct,
or a forbearing father, longing to forgive.
This then is what I ask, O Font of pity,
trusting in your almighty mercy
and your merciful might;
I ask you, by the power of your most sweet
name, and by your holy manhood's
mystery,
to put away my sins and heal the languors
of my soul,
mindful only of your goodness, not of my
ingratitude.
Lord, may your good, sweet Spirit
descend into my heart,
and fashion there a dwelling for himself,
cleansing it from all defilement
both of flesh and spirit,
inpouring into it
the increment of faith and hope and love,
disposing it to penitence and love and
gentleness.

May he quench with the dew of his
blessings
the heat of my desires,
and with this power put to death
my carnal impulses and fleshly lusts.
In labors, and in watchings, and in fastings
may he afford me fervor and discretion,
to love and praise you,
to pray and thank you;
and may he give me power and devotion
to order every act and thought
according to your will
and also perseverance in these virtues
unto my life's end.
Amen.

PRAYERS OF SAINT FRANCIS OF ASSISI

The Prayer for Peace

Lord, make me an instrument of your
peace.
Where there is hatred, let me sow love;
where there is injury, pardon;
where there is doubt, faith;
where there is despair, hope;
where there is darkness, light;

where there is sadness, joy.
O Divine Master, grant that I may not so
much seek
to be consoled, as to console;
to be understood, as to understand;
to be loved, as to love.
For it is in giving that we receive;
it is in pardoning that we are pardoned;
and it is in dying that we are born to
eternal life.

The Canticle of Brother Sun

Most High, omnipotent, good Lord,
to you alone belong praise and glory,
honor and blessing,
no man is worthy to breathe your name.

Be praised, my Lord, for all your creatures.

In the first place for the blessed Brother
Sun,
who gives us the day and enlightens us
through you.
He is beautiful and radiant with his great
splendor.
Giving witness to you, most Omnipotent
One.
Be praised, my Lord, for Sister Moon and
the stars

formed by you so bright, precious, and
   beautiful.

Be praised, my Lord, for Brother Wind
and the airy skies, so cloudy and serene;
for every weather, be praised, for it is life-
   giving.

Be praised, my Lord, for Sister Water,
so necessary, yet so precious, humble, and
   chaste.

Be praised, my Lord, for Brother Fire,
who lights up the night.
He is beautiful and carefree, robust and
   fierce.

Be praised, my Lord, for our sister, Mother
   Earth,
who nourishes and watches us
while bringing forth abundance of fruits
with colored flowers and herbs.

Be praised, my Lord, for those who pardon
   through your love
and bear weaknesses and trial.
Blessed are those who endure in peace,
for they will be crowned by you, Most
   High.

Be praised, my Lord, for our sister, Bodily
   Death,

whom no living man can escape.
Woe to those who die in sin.
Blessed are those who discover your holy
   will.
The second death will do them no harm.

Praise and bless the Lord.
Render thanks.
Serve him with great humility. Amen.

PRAYER OF SAINT THOMAS AQUINAS

Grant me, O Lord my God, a mind to
know you, a heart to seek you, wisdom to
find you, conduct pleasing to you, faithful
perseverance in waiting for you, and a
hope of finally embracing you. Amen.

PRAYER OF SAINT BRIDGET OF SWEDEN

O Jesus! King most loving and desir-
able, remember the grief which you did
suffer when, naked and like a common
criminal, you were raised and fastened to
the cross, when all your relatives and
friends abandoned you, except your beloved Mother, who remained close to you
during your agony. You did entrust her to

your faithful disciple when you said, "Woman, behold your son. Behold your Mother." I beg you, O my Savior, by the sword of sorrow which pierced the soul of your holy Mother, to have compassion on me in all my affliction and tribulations, both corporal and spiritual, and to assist me in all my trials, and especially at the hour of my death. Amen.

PRAYER OF SAINT NICHOLAS OF CUSA

Thank you, Jesus, for bringing me this far. In your light I see the light of my life. Your teaching is brief and to the point. You persuade us to trust in our heavenly Father. You command us to love one another. What is easier than to believe in God? What is sweeter than to love him? Your yoke is pleasant, your burden is light, you, the one and only Teacher! You promise everything to those who obey your teaching; you ask nothing too hard for a believer, nothing a lover can refuse. Your promises to your disciples are true, entirely true; nothing but the truth. Even more, you promise us yourself, the perfection of all that can be made perfect. Thank you, Jesus, now and always. Amen.

PRAYER OF SAINT CATHERINE OF SIENA

O great God in whom all perfections are infinite, I adore, praise, glorify, and love you. My heart overflows at the contemplation of your beauty and splendor. I rejoice that you are so perfect and holy and I desire to participate in your perfections to the degree that will give you the most glory.

I desire to forget myself by the contemplation of your attributes and I ask that you fill me with these perfections more and more each day that I may radiate your Son through the Holy Spirit. Amen.

PRAYER OF SAINT THOMAS MORE

Lord, grant me a holy heart that sees always what is fine and pure and is not frightened at the sight of sin, but creates order wherever it goes. Grant me a heart that knows nothing of boredom, weeping, and sighing. Let me not be too concerned with the bothersome thing I call "myself." Lord, give me a sense of humor and I will find happiness in life and profit for others.

PRAYERS OF SAINT IGNATIUS LOYOLA

Lord, I freely yield all my freedom to you. Take my memory, my intellect, and my entire will. You have given me anything I am or have; I give it all back to you to stand under your will alone. Your love and your grace are enough for me; I shall ask for nothing more.

*   *   *

Teach us, Lord, to serve you as you deserve; to give and not to count the cost; to fight and not to heed the wounds; to toil and not to seek rest; to labor and not ask for any reward save that of knowing that we do your will. Amen.

PRAYER OF AN AMERICAN INDIAN

O Great Spirit, whose voice I hear in the winds, and whose breath gives life to all the world, hear me. I am small and weak. I need your strength and wisdom.

Let me walk in beauty and make my eyes ever behold the red and purple sunset.

Make my hands respect the things you have made.

Make my ears sharp to hear your voice.

Make me wise so that I may understand the things you have taught your people.

Let me learn the lessons you have hidden in every leaf and rock.

I seek strength, not to be greater than my brother, but to fight my greatest enemy—myself.

Make me always ready to come to you with clean hands and straight eyes.

So when life fades, as the fading sunset, my spirit may come to you without shame.

PRAYER OF SAINT JOHN BAPTIST DE LA SALLE

O my God, I beg you to grant me peace with my neighbor, for I cannot enjoy your favor if I do not live in union with my brothers and sisters. I can preserve this union by mildness and patience. Give me, then, I beseech you, these two virtues. Grant that I may always speak and act kindly toward all, that I may suffer patiently for you whatever wrongs, injuries, and insults may be done to me. May I not be angered or displeased with anything but rather may I suffer patiently whatever happens to me from others. Amen.

PRAYERS OF CARDINAL NEWMAN

To be Christ in the World

Note: This prayer has been widely distributed by Mother Teresa of Calcutta

Dear Lord, help me to spread thy fragrance everywhere I go. Flood my soul with thy spirit and life. Penetrate and possess my whole being so utterly that all my life may only be a radiance of thine. Shine through me, and be so in me that every soul I come in contact with may feel thy presence in my soul.

Let them look up and see no longer me—but only thee, O Lord! Stay with me, then I shall begin to shine as thou dost; so to shine as to be a light to others.

The light, O Lord, will be all from thee, none of it will be mine, it will be thou shining on others through me.

Let me thus praise thee in the way thou dost love best, by shining on those around me.

Let me preach thee without preaching, not by words but by my example, by the catching force, the sympathetic influence of what I do, the evident fullness of the love my heart bears to thee. Amen.

Lead, Kindly Light

Lead, Kindly Light, amid the encircling
  gloom,
  Lead thou me on!
The night is dark and I am far from
  home—

Lead thou me on!
Keep thou my feet, I do not ask to see
The distant scene—one step enough for
    me.
I was not ever thus, nor pray'd that thou
    Shouldst lead me on!
I loved to choose and see my path, but now
    Lead thou me on!
I loved the garish day, and spite of fears,
Pride ruled my will: remember not past
    years.
So long Thy power hast blest me, sure it
    still
    Will lead me on,
O'er moor and fen, o'er crag and torrent
    till
    The night is gone;
And with the morn those angel faces smile
Which I have loved long since and lost
    awhile.

PRAYERS OF SAINT THÉRÈSE OF LISIEUX

O my God, I ask of you for myself and
for those whom I hold dear the grace to
fulfill perfectly your holy will, to accept
for love of you the joys and sufferings of
this passing life, so that we may one day

be united in heaven for all eternity. Amen.

Oblation of Love

That my life may be one act of perfect love, I offer myself as a victim of holocaust to your merciful love, imploring you to consume me unceasingly, and to allow the floods of infinite tenderness pent up in you to overflow into my soul, that I may become a very martyr of your love, O my God! May this martyrdom, after having prepared me to appear in your presence, free me from this life at last, and may my soul take its flight, without delay, into the embrace of your merciful love.

O my beloved, I desire at every beat of my heart to renew this offering an infinite number of times, until the shadows flee away and everlastingly I can tell you my love face to face. Amen.

PRAYER OF ABANDONMENT OF CHARLES DE FOUCAULD

Father, I abandon myself into your hands; do with me what you will. What-

ever you may do, I thank you. I am ready
for all, I accept all. Let only your will be
done in me and in all your creation—I
wish no more than this, O Lord. Into your
hands I commend my soul, I offer it to
you with all the love of my heart, for I
love you, Lord, and so need to give myself, to surrender myself into your hands,
without reserve, and with boundless confidence, for you are my Father.

PRAYER OF ROBERT LOUIS STEVENSON

Purge out of every heart the lurking
　　grudge.
Give us grace and strength to forbear and
　　so persevere.
Offenders, give us the grace to accept and
　　forgive offenders.
Forgetful of ourselves, help us to bear
　　cheerfully the forgetfulness of others.
Give us courage and gaiety and the quiet
　　mind.
Spare us to our friends, soften us to our
　　enemies.
Bless us, if it may be, in all our innocent
　　endeavors.
If it may not, give us the strength to
　　encounter that which is to come,

that we may be brave in peril,
temperate in wrath,
and in all changes in fortune,
and down to the gates of death,
loyal and loving to one another.

PRAYER OF THOMAS MERTON

My Lord God, I have no idea where I am going. I do not see the road ahead of me. I cannot know for certain where it will end. Nor do I really know myself, and the fact that I think that I am following your will does not mean that I am actually doing so. But I believe that the desire to please you does in fact please you. And I hope I have that desire in all that I am doing. I hope that I will never do anything apart from that desire. And I know that as I do this you will lead me by the right road though I may know nothing about it. Therefore will I trust you always though I may seem to be lost and in the shadow of death. I will not fear, for you are ever with me, and you will never leave me to face my perils alone.

PRAYER OF PIERRE TEILHARD DE CHARDIN

Lord God, when I go up to your altar for communion, grant that I may derive from it a discernment of the infinite perspectives hidden beneath the smallness and closeness of the host within which you are concealed. Already I have accustomed myself to recognize beneath the inertness of the morsel of bread a consuming power which, as the greatest doctors of your Church have said, far from being absorbed into me, absorbs me into itself. Help me now to overcome that remaining illusion which would make me think of you as touching me only in a limited and momentary way.

I begin to understand: under the sacramental species you touch me first of all through the "accidents" of matter, of the material bread; but then, in consequence of this, you touch me also through the entire universe inasmuch as the entire universe, thanks to that primary influence, ebbs and flows over me. In a true sense, the arms and the heart which you open to me are nothing less than all the united powers of the world which, permeated through and through by your will, your inclinations, your temperament, bend over my being or form it and feed it and draw it into the blazing center of your infinite fire. In the host, Lord Jesus, you offer me my life.

PRAYERS OF KARL RAHNER

Prayer for Fulfillment

O Lord, when shall I once and for all grasp this, this law of your life and so of my life? The law that death is life; losing oneself is finding oneself, poverty is riches and suffering is a grace, that to reach the end in truth is fulfillment.

* * *

An Opening Prayer

I should like to speak to you about my prayer, O Lord. And though it often seems to me that you pay little heed to what I try to say to you in my prayers, please listen carefully to me now.

PRAYER OF MOTHER TERESA OF CALCUTTA

Dear Jesus, help me to spread your fragrance everywhere I go. Flood my soul with your spirit and life. Penetrate and possess my whole being so utterly that all my life may only be a radiance of yours. Shine through me, and be so in me that every soul I come in contact with may feel your presence in my soul.

Let them look up and see no longer me—but only Jesus. Stay with me. Then I shall begin to shine as you do: so to shine as to be a light to others.

The light, O Jesus, will be all from you, none of it will be mine; it will be you shining on others through me.

Let me thus praise you in the way you love best, by shining on those around me.

Let me preach you without preaching, not by words but by my example, by the catching force, the sympathetic influence of what I do, the evident fullness of the love my heart bears to you. Amen.

PRAYER OF HENRI NOUWEN

God, give me the courage to be revolutionary as your Son Jesus Christ was. Give me the courage to loosen myself from this world. Teach me to stand up free and to shun no criticism. God, it is for your kingdom. Make me free, make me poor in this world. Then will I be rich in the real world, which this life is all about. God, thank you for the vision of the future, but make it fact and not theory.

11

Prayers for Particular Occasions

PRAYERS BEFORE COMMUNION

Act of Faith

Lord Jesus Christ, I firmly believe that you are present in this blessed Sacrament, as true God and true man, with your Body and Blood, your soul and divinity. My Redeemer and my Judge, I adore your divine majesty together with the angels and saints. I believe, O Lord; increase my faith.

Act of Hope

Good Jesus, in you alone I place all my hope. You are my salvation and my strength, the Source of all good. Through your mercy, through your Passion and

Death, I hope to obtain the pardon of my sins, the grace of final perseverance, and a happy eternity.

Act of Love

Jesus, my God, I love you with my whole heart and above all things, because you are the one supreme Good and an infinitely perfect God. You have given your life for me, a poor sinner, and in your mercy you have even offered yourself as food for my soul. My God, I love you. Inflame my heart so that I may love you more.

Act of Contrition

O my Savior, I am truly sorry for having offended you because you are infinitely good and sin displeases you. I detest all the sins of my life and I desire to atone for them. Through the merits of your Precious Blood, wash from me all stain of sin, so that, cleansed, I may worthily approach the Most Holy Sacrament of the Altar.

Act of Desire

Jesus, my God and my all, I long for you. My heart yearns to receive you in Holy Communion. Come, Bread of heaven and Food of angels, to nourish me and to rejoice my heart. Come, most lovable Friend, to enflame me with such love that I may never again be separated from you.

PRAYERS AFTER COMMUNION

Act of Thanksgiving

From the depths of my heart I thank you, dear Lord, for your infinite kindness in coming to me. How good you are to me! With your Mother and all the saints and angels, I praise your mercy and generosity toward me, a sinner. I thank you for nourishing me with your Sacred Body and your Precious Blood. I will try to show my gratitude to you by obedience to your commandments, by fidelity to my duties, by kindness to my neighbors, and by an earnest endeavor to become more like you in my daily conduct.

Prayer of Saint Thomas Aquinas

Lord, Father all-powerful and ever-living God, I thank you, for even though I am a sinner, your unprofitable servant, not because of my worth but in the kindness of your mercy, you have fed me with the precious Body and Blood of your Son, our Lord Jesus Christ. I pray that this communion may not bring me condemnation and punishment but forgiveness and salvation. May it be a helmet of faith and a shield of good will. May it purify me from evil ways and put an end to my evil passions. May it bring me charity and patience, humility and obedience, and growth in the power to do good. May it be my strong defense against all my enemies, visible and invisible, and the perfect calming of all my evil impulses, bodily and spiritual. May it unite me more closely to you, the one true God, and lead me safely through death to everlasting happiness with you. I pray that you will lead me, a sinner, to the banquet where you, with your Son and Holy Spirit, are true and perfect light, total fulfillment, everlasting joy, gladness without end, and perfect happiness to your saints. Grant this through Christ our Lord. Amen.

Prayer to Our Redeemer

(The *Anima Christi*)

Soul of Christ, sanctify me.
Body of Christ, save me.
Blood of Christ, inebriate me.
Water from the side of Christ, wash me.
Passion of Christ, strengthen me.
O good Jesus, hear me;
within your wounds hide me.
From the malicious enemy defend me.
In the hour of death call me,
and bid me to come to thee
that with thy saints I might praise thee
forever and ever. Amen.

Prayer to Jesus Crucified

O good and gentle Jesus, I kneel before you, asking you most earnestly to enkindle within my heart a deep and lively faith, hope, and charity, with true repentance for my sins and a firm resolve to make amends. As I reflect upon your five wounds and dwell upon them with deep compassion and sorrow, I recall the words your prophet David spoke long ago of you: They have pierced my hands and my feet, they have numbered all my bones.

Prayer to the Blessed Virgin Mary

Mary, I come to you with childlike confidence and earnestly beg you to take me under your powerful protection. Grant me a place in your loving motherly heart. Help me to worthily thank my Lord, your Son, for coming to me in Holy Communion. I place myself in your hands and give you my own heart. Amen.

PRAYERS BEFORE THE SACRAMENT OF RECONCILIATION

Receive my confession, O most loving and gracious Lord, Jesus Christ, only hope for salvation. Grant to me true contrition so that I may make due satisfaction for my sins. O Savior of the world, you gave yourself on the cross to save sinners. Look upon me a sinner, have pity on me, and give me the light to know my sins, true sorrow for them, and a firm purpose to avoid them in the future.

O gracious Mother Mary, Mother of Jesus, I implore you by your powerful in-

tercession to obtain these graces for me
from your divine Son.

PRAYER ON A DAY OF FASTING

Father, I am hungry. The day has
been a long one. The thought of food
keeps coming to mind, and I have even
debated about breaking this fast because
it hurts so much to be hungry. But, more
than that, it is the whole feeling of weakness and even a little unavoidable sadness
that comes with an empty stomach. I am
not asking you to take away the pain but
just give me the strength to endure it
with a generous heart, because I keep
thinking about my brothers and sisters,
some of them little children, who have
nothing to eat this day and may die even
before tomorrow. Show them your
mercy, Father, and please forgive me.
Teach us all how to share so that no one
hungers at your table. Amen.

PRAYERS FOR SATURDAY EVENING

O God, thank you for having brought
us safely through this week. You have
kept us well, provided for us, and en-

abled us to do something of meaning with our time. May you continue to show us your blessings. Protect your people, allow them to prosper. Help our enemies to understand that the way to fulfillment is with decency, good will, and a desire for cooperation. Help people all over the world to come closer to peace. Ease their fears, soften their desperation, and help them begin to find solutions. Grant us all health, contentment, and peace.

* * *

Holy One of Blessing, your Presence fills creation. You have made us holy with your commandments and delighted in us. In love, you have favored us with the gift of your holy Sabbath, a heritage which recalls the deed of creation. It is the first day among holy days, reminding us of our going forth from Egypt. You gave us your holy Sabbath as a treasure to grace all our generations. Holy One of Blessing, you make the Sabbath holy.

—adapted from the Jewish tradition

PRAYER ON A BIRTHDAY

Father, Source of all life and health and happiness, hear our prayer. May your servant who is celebrating a birthday be abundantly blessed. As we thank you for this gift of another year of life, we ask for many happy years, all of them pleasing to you. We ask this through Christ our Lord. Amen.

PRAYER ON A WEDDING ANNIVERSARY

Lord, you worked your first sign, a joyful one of abundant and good wine, at a wedding feast, to show how you delight in married life. We thank you for the gift of this vocation, this sacrament, this life together. May the years be multiplied, and their joys even more so. May this marital love be a true witness to your love for us, your Church. May the graces of this marriage help us to attain the eternal nuptial feast in your Kingdom. We praise and thank you, with your Father and Holy Spirit, this day and always. Amen.

PRAYER AT THE BEGINNING OF A JOURNEY

O God our Father, you led your servant Abraham from his home and guarded him in all his wanderings. Guide and guard us now as we go forth in your name. Protect us from storms, from weariness, from trouble and danger. With this protection, may we reach our destination [and return safely home again]. Amen.

PRAYER AT THE END OF A JOURNEY

Blessed are you, O Lord our God, for you have been with us in all our ways and have brought us safely to our destination. We thank you for a safe journey. Keep us in your care through all life's pilgrimage until we find our eternal home with you in heaven. Amen.

PRAYER IN TIME OF SICKNESS

Praised be you, O Christ, for your kindness and fidelity and the humble acceptance of sufferings for our salvation. Through the strength of your loving Spirit help me to shoulder my infirmities and be at peace in the knowledge that in union with your death on the cross I may also participate in the glories of your resurrection for all eternity. Amen.

PRAYER IN THE MIDST OF TEMPTATION

Lord, you were like us in all things but sin. You knew temptation in the wilderness. You knew what it was to feel abandoned. I now feel myself mightily drawn toward sin and away from your loving company. You seem to have already left me. Lord, I cry out to you. Be with me now in this hour of trial. Help me to be faithful to you and to your love even as you were faithful to me, even to the point of dying for me on the Cross.

Holy Mary, holy Mother, pray for me now.

Holy Guardian Angels, help me now.

AT THE MOMENT OF DEATH— ROMAN RITUAL

Go forth, Christian soul, from this world in the name of God the Father, who created you, in the name of Jesus Christ, Son of the living God, who suffered for you, in the name of the Holy Spirit, who was poured out upon you, go forth, faithful Christian.

May you live in peace this day, may your home be with God in Zion, with Mary, the Virgin Mother of God, with Joseph, and all the angels and saints.

I commend you, our dear one, to Almighty God, and entrust you to your Creator. May you return to him who formed you from the dust of the earth. May holy Mary, the angels, and the saints come to meet you as you go forth from life. May Christ who was crucified for you bring you freedom and peace. May Christ who died for you admit you into his garden of paradise. May Christ, the true Shepherd, acknowledge you as one of his flock. May he forgive all your sins, and set you among those he has chosen. May you see your Redeemer face to face and enjoy the vision of God forever. Amen.

PRAYER AT THE DEATH OF A CHILD

The Lord gives and the Lord takes away; blessed be the name of the Lord. Lord, you know how difficult it is for us to bless you in this time of loss. The death of any person is a tragedy, but the death of an innocent little one cuts us deeply. Lord, give us the grace to say: Thy will be done. And to believe truly that this is the working of your mysterious love. Renew our faith and hope so that the promised reunion in eternal life may be real for us in this time of loss. Lord, you who so loved little ones, take care of our little one and bring us all together to life eternal. Amen.

PRAYER DURING THE TIME OF MOURNING

God our Father, God of all consolation, in your unending love and mercy for us, you turn the darkness of death into the dawn of a new life. Show now your compassion for us in our sorrow. Be our refuge and our strength to lift us from the darkness of our grief to the peace and light of your healing presence. Your Son, our Lord Jesus, by dying for us, conquered death and by rising again, restored life. May we go forward confidently, knowing that after this pilgrimage we will be reunited with all those whom we love, in your home where every tear will be wiped away. We ask this through Jesus in the Holy Spirit of Love. Amen.

12

Prayers for Particular Concerns

PRAYER FOR FAITH, HOPE, AND LOVE

Father, we know that you are more ready to give what is best for us than we are to receive it. So, in full confidence, we ask you to increase our faith, strengthen our hope, and enkindle our love for you and for all your children, our sisters and brothers. We ask this through your Son, our Brother, Jesus Christ our Lord. Amen.

PRAYER FOR LIGHT

O Holy Spirit of God, take me as your disciple. Guide me, illumine me, sanctify me. Bind my hands, that they may do no evil. Cover my eyes, that they may see it no more. Sanctify my heart, that evil may not dwell within me. Be my God, be my guide. Wherever you lead me, I will go. Whatever you forbid me, I will renounce. And whatever you command me, in your strength I will do. Lead me, then, unto the fullness of your truth. Amen.

PRAYER FOR PEACE AND JUSTICE

Almighty and eternal God, may your grace enkindle in all of us a love for the many unfortunate people whom poverty and misery reduce to a condition of life unworthy of human beings. Arouse in the hearts of those who call you Father a hunger and thirst for justice and peace and for fraternal charity in deeds and in truth. Grant, O Lord, peace in our days, peace to souls, peace to families, peace to our country, and peace among nations. Amen.

—Pope Pius XII

PRAYER FOR PATIENCE

O blessed Jesus, give me stillness of soul in you. Let your mighty calmness reign in me. Rule me, O King of gentleness, King of peace.

Give me control, great power of self-control; control over my words, thoughts, actions. From all irritability, want of meekness, want of gentleness, dear Lord, deliver me. By your own deep patience, give me patience and stillness of soul in you. Make me in this, and in all, more and more like you. Amen.

PRAYER TO BE A GOOD CITIZEN

Lord Jesus Christ, our hope and our savior, in history you were the subject of a mighty empire, a lowly member of a conquered and occupied nation. You understand the dangers of being a political person, the challenge of serving God and Caesar both. Help us to discover our higher loyalties in the daily fulfillment of our lesser obligations. Give us the insight and courage to criticize where necessary and the grace to love and serve one another in the here and now as citizens of our country and of the world. Establish the reign of God in our hearts and bring us to full citizenship in the Kingdom of

Heaven, where you live and reign forever and ever. Amen.

PRAYER FOR HUMAN SOLIDARITY

Father, you have made us red, yellow, brown, white, and black; tall and short, fat and thin, rich and poor, young and old—all human persons are your children. Teach us to cooperate rather than to compete, to respect rather than to revile, to forgive rather than condemn. Your Son turned from no one. May we learn, like him, to be open to the share of the divine that you have implanted in each of your daughters and sons. And may we forge a bond of love that will make a living reality the unity of the human family which we profess under your loving and universal Fatherhood. Amen.

PRAYER FOR THE PLANET

Here we are, Lord—a planet at prayer. Attune our spirits that we may hear your harmonies and bow before your creative power, that we may face our violent discords and join with your

Energy to make heard in every heart your hymn of peace.

Here we are, Lord—a militarized planet. Transform our fears that we may transform our war fields into wheat fields, arms into handshakes, missiles into messengers of peace.

Here we are, Lord—a polluted planet. Purify our vision that we may perceive ways to purify our beloved lands, cleanse our precious waters, de-smog our life-giving air.

Here we are, Lord—an exploited planet. Heal our hearts, Lord, that we may respect our resources, hold priceless our people, and provide for our starving children an abundance of daily bread.

—Joan Metzner, MM

PRAYER FOR THE HUNGRY OF THE WORLD

Father, in your wisdom you have made us dependent on one another, and so we pray for the starving millions in our world. Give us true repentance for our greed and selfishness. Empower us to make amends as best we can. Help us to find the ways to share so that no one hungers at the table of life. We ask this through Christ our Lord. Amen.

PRAYER FOR OUR PARISH

O God, you have made us the Church of your Son. Make our parish a family of one heart and one mind in love toward you. Grant that our common life and witness may be an example to all about us. Guide our pastor and his assistants in their ministry. Listen to the prayers of [the patron of the parish], our patron, and keep us secure in your love. Teach us to reach out to other parishes less fortunate. Give us a great love for all the Church, for our Holy Father, for our bishop, and all those who serve. Help us to be a leaven of joy and peace within the human family. Bring us all together to life eternal. Amen.

EMMAUS PRAYER FOR PRIESTS

Lord Jesus, hear our prayer for the spiritual renewal of priests. We praise you for their ministry to the Church. Renew them with the gifts of your Spirit.

You once opened the Scriptures to your disciples on the road to Emmaus. Now renew your ordained ministers with the truth and power of your Word.

In the Eucharist, you gave the Emmaus disciples renewed life and hope. Nourish priests with your own Body and Blood. Help them to imitate in their lives the death and resurrection they celebrate at the altar.

Give priests enthusiasm for the Gospel, zeal for the salvation of all, courage in leadership, humility in service, fellowship with one another and with all their brothers and sisters in you.

For you love them, Lord Jesus, and we love and pray for them in your Name. Amen.

PRAYER FOR THE MISSIONS

God of Truth, Father, Son, and Holy Spirit, hear our prayer for those who do not know you, that your Name may be praised among all peoples of the world. Sustain and inspire your servants who bring them the Gospel. Bring fresh vigor to wavering faith; sustain our faith when it is still fragile. Renew our missionary zeal. Make us witnesses to your love, full of love, of strength, and of faith, for your glory and for the salvation of the world. Amen.

PRAYER FOR BISHOPS

Father, Shepherd of your flock, there is so much to set right, so many dangers to avert, such an enormous task of giving witness to you before the world. As we bring our needs to you, we bring also those of our bishops. May you strengthen and preserve them, enlighten and guide them in the way of true love and service, for your glory and the well-being of us all. We ask this through Jesus Christ our Lord. Amen.

PRAYER FOR THE POPE

Let us pray for our Holy Father, Pope John Paul.

The Lord preserve him and give him life, and make him blessed upon the earth, and deliver him not to the will of his enemies. Amen.

PRAYER FOR THE CHURCH

Gracious Father, we pray to you for your holy Catholic Church. Fill it with your truth. Keep it in your peace. Where it is corrupt, reform it. Where it is in error, correct it. Where it is right, defend it. Where it is in want, provide for it. Where it is divided, reunite it, for the sake of your Son, our Lord, Jesus Christ. Amen.

—William Laud

PRAYER FOR VOCATIONS TO THE RELIGIOUS AND MONASTIC LIFE

Father, you have told us that to know and love you is eternal life and that that life has begun in us already through your Son's victory over sin and death. This is the faith that fills cloisters and declares to all your unimaginable goodness. We pray that men and women may be drawn more and more to these schools of your service. We ask this through Jesus Christ, your Son. Amen.

PRAYER FOR SPIRITUAL GROWTH

Father, you are able to accomplish immeasurably more than we can ask or imagine. Make us grasp fully, together with all the saints, the breadth and the length, the height and the depth of Christ's love, which surpasses all knowledge, in order that we may be completely filled with the utter fullness of God. Father, grant us, out of your riches, to be strengthened through the Spirit for the development of our inner selves, and to have Christ dwelling through faith in our hearts, and to be rooted and grounded in love. We ask this through our Lord, Jesus Christ, your Son. Amen.

—adapted from Ephesians 3

PRAYER BEFORE STUDY

Creator of all things, true source of light and wisdom, origin of all being, graciously let a ray of your light penetrate into the darkness of my understanding. Take from me the double darkness in which I have been born, an obscurity of sin and ignorance. Give me a keen understanding, a retentive memory, and the ability to grasp things correctly and fundamentally. Grant me the talent of being exact in my explanations and the ability to express myself with thoroughness and charm. Point out the beginning, direct the progress, and help in the completion. I ask this through Christ our Lord. Amen.

—Saint Thomas Aquinas

PRAYER FOR VOCATIONAL DISCERNMENT

Lord God, you promised strength to all those who would follow your will, but my problem is that I don't know what it is. Your world holds so many possibilities for me.

After seriously assessing my potential, I still hesitate to choose one definite way of life. Inspire my decision that I may fully live out whatever commitment I choose for your greater glory and the happiness of those whose lives I touch. Help me to make the most of the life you have given me. In this way, I will radiate your gifts to all who take time to see. I ask you this in the name of Jesus, my Brother. Amen.

PRAYER FOR A HAPPY MARRIAGE

Heavenly Father, from the very beginning you wanted men and women to find love and create new life in marriage. Marriage is a mystery of your love for us and of our faithful love for each other. Help us to give ourselves seriously to a marriage in Christ who calls us to a union of true affection and strengthens our resolves in the sacrament of matrimony. Give us sensitive hearts, discerning minds, and ready wills, eager to serve you and to discover the truth of each other. Nourish our sexuality and direct it to good. On our wedding day unite us [you united us] before your altar, feed us with the Body and Blood of your Christ and become the common center of our hearts and our home. Amen.

PRAYER FOR FRUITFULNESS

Lord, it was by your grace and goodness that we have been bound together in the holy covenant of matrimony. Our love is to be a sign of your love for your Church. Even as you wish your holy

Church to be fruitful and bear many children unto life eternal, so in your great mercy, bless our union and make it fruitful, so that we may have the joy of being with you co-creators of life. Bless our home with children. And help us by your grace to so raise them that they will ever be a benediction to our name and worthy sons and daughters of you, their heavenly Father.

PRAYER FOR THE FAMILY

O God of goodness and mercy, to your fatherly protection we commend our family, our household, and all that belongs to us. We commit all to your Love and keeping. Fill this house with your blessing even as you filled the holy house of Nazareth with your Presence.

Keep far from us, above all else, the taint of sin, and reign in our midst by your law, by your love, and by the exercise of every virtue. Let each one of us obey you, love you, and set ourselves to imitate in our own lives your example, that of Mary, your Mother and our Mother most loving, and that of your guardian, Saint Joseph.

Preserve us and our house from all evils and misfortunes, but grant that we may be ever resigned to your divine will even in the sorrows which it shall please you to send us. Finally give to all of us the grace to live in perfect harmony and in the fullness of love toward each other and our neighbors. Grant that every one of us may deserve by a holy life the comfort of your sacraments at the hour of death. O Jesus, bless us and protect us.

O Mary, Mother of grace and of mercy, defend us against the wicked spirit, reconcile us with your Son, commit us to his keeping so that we may be made worthy of his promises.

Saint Joseph, foster father of our Savior, guardian of his holy Mother, head of the Holy Family, intercede for us, bless us, and defend our home at all times.

Saint Michael, defend us against the wicked cunning of the powers of hell.

Saint Gabriel, make us to understand the holy will of God.

Saint Raphael, keep us free from all sickness and from every danger to our lives.

Our holy Guardian Angels, keep our feet safely on the path of salvation both day and night.

Our holy Patrons, pray for us before the throne of God.

Bless this house, O God our Father, who has created us; O God the Son, who has suffered for us upon the cross; and Holy Spirit, who has sanctified us in holy baptism. May the one God in three divine Persons preserve our bodies, purify our minds, direct our hearts, and bring us all to everlasting life.

Glory be to the Father, glory be to the Son, glory be to the Holy Spirit. Amen.

PRAYER FOR THOSE IN TROUBLE

Lord, you are present everywhere. We ask your help for those who are in trouble. Where they are at odds with each other, we pray for a breakthrough and reconciliation. Where a job has been lost, grant a new opportunity for useful work. Where there is sickness, we pray for healing and strength. Where there are patterns which make life dull, we pray for a broken routine which will al-

low new possibilities. O Lord, some are
deeply troubled. We ask you to help them
and to help us to know what to do. We ask
this through the compassion of your Son,
our Lord and Teacher. Amen.

PRAYERS FOR A FRIEND

May Yahweh answer you in time of trouble,
may the Name of the God of Jacob protect
  you!

May he send you help from the sanctuary,
give you support from Zion,
remember all your offerings
and find your sacrifices acceptable;
may he grant you your heart's desire,
and crown all your plans with success;
may we shout with joy for your victory,
and plant our banners under the name of
  our God!

May Yahweh grant all your petitions!

—Psalm 20 [19]

*　　*　　*

Lord God, we can hope for others
nothing better than the happiness we desire for ourselves. Therefore, I pray you,
do not separate me after death from

those I have tenderly loved on earth.
Grant that where I am they may be with
me, and that I may enjoy their presence
in heaven after being so often deprived
of it on earth. Lord God, I ask you to
receive your beloved children into your
life-giving heart. After this brief life on
earth, give them eternal happiness.
Amen.

—Saint Ambrose of Milan

PRAYER FOR HEALING

Lord, you have told us to ask and we will
　　receive,
　　　　to seek and we will find,
　　　　to knock and you will open the door to
　　　　　　us.

I trust in your love for me
　　and in the healing power of your
　　　　compassion.
I praise you and thank you for the mercy
　　you have shown to me.

Lord, I am sorry for all my sins.
I ask for your help in renouncing the sinful
　　patterns of my life.
I accept with all my heart your forgiving
　　love.

And I ask for the grace to be aware
   of the disorders that exist within
      myself.
Let me not offend you by my weak human
   nature
      or by my impatience, resentment, or
         neglect
      of people who are a part of my life.
Rather, teach me the gift of understanding
   and the ability to forgive, just as you
      continue to forgive me.

I seek your strength and your peace so that
   I may become
      your instrument in sharing those gifts
         with others.

Guide me in my prayer that I might know
   what needs to be healed
      and how to ask you for that healing.

It is you, Lord, whom I seek.
Please enter the door of my heart
   and fill me with the presence of your
      Spirit now and forever.

I thank you, Lord, for doing this.   Amen.

—Fr. Ralph A. Di Orio

PRAYER FOR THE DYING

Lord, this day some will be gathered to the Father. Grant that they may go forth with caring ones about them, without terrible pain of body, with clarity of mind and heart, and with a joyful expectancy of soul. May your holy Mother be with them to comfort and strengthen them at the last. May your holy angels lead them into their heavenly home. Amen.

PRAYERS FOR THE DECEASED

O God, Creator and Redeemer of all, give to your servant(s) departed this life full remission of all her/his (their) offenses, that s/he (they) may obtain your pardon and so enter into the fullness of eternal joy. We ask this through Christ our Lord.

Eternal rest grant unto them, O Lord.
And let perpetual light shine upon them.
May they rest in peace.
Amen.

* * *

Lord, remember N. In baptism he (she) died with Christ; may he (she) also share his resurrection, when Christ will raise our mortal bodies and make them like his own in glory. Welcome into your kingdom our departed brothers and sisters, and all who have died in your friendship. There we hope to share in your glory when every tear will be wiped away. On that day we shall see you, our God, as you are. We shall become like you and praise you forever through Christ our Lord, from whom all good things come. Amen.

13

❧ ✦ ❧

Prayers of
General Intercession

O God of unchangeable power and
eternal light, look favorably on your
whole Church, that wonderful and sacred mystery, and by the tranquil opera-
tion of your perpetual providence carry
out the work of our salvation; and let the
whole world feel and see that things
which were cast down are being raised
up; that things which had grown old are
being made new; and that all things are
returning to perfection through him
from whom they took their origin, our
Lord Jesus Christ, who lives and reigns
with you and Holy Spirit, one God, world
without end. Amen.

—Gelasian Sacramentary

*   *   *

Lord God, who brings judgment to the earth that we may repent, who in Christ did show Love's mercy and renewed our lives, receive the prayer of those who live in Christ, united in his sacrifice, to draw all things to be for him. In these dark days, when men exalt themselves to be the measure of the universe, Lord God, accept our penitence that we may know ourselves and die to self that in Christ we may respond to the command: Be perfect. May we grow in knowledge and in willingness to serve and to live in him, that his grace, love's unity increasing, may unite all Christian people into a visible witness of Church and faith, in a unity of sacrifice, to draw all to redirect their lives to God.

—Gilbert Shaw

14

℔ ❦ ℔

Brief Prayers —
Ejaculations —
Aspirations

PRAYERS FROM THE GOSPELS

Be it done unto me according to your
    word.

Thy will be done.

Lord, increase my faith.

Lord, I believe; help my unbelief.

Father, not my will but yours be done.

Father, into your hands I commend my
    spirit.

My Lord and my God.

OTHER PRAYERS FROM THE SACRED SCRIPTURES

Create in me a clean heart, O God, and put a new and right spirit in me.

Keep me, O Lord, as the apple of your eye.

O God, come to my assistance; O Lord, make haste to help me.

O Lord, reward us not according to our sins which we have done, neither according to our iniquities.

O Praise the Lord, all you nations; praise him all you peoples, for his mercy is confirmed upon us and the truth of the Lord remains forever.

Blessing and glory and wisdom and thanksgiving, honor, might, and power be unto our God forever and ever. Amen.

FOR ADVENT

Divine Babe of Bethlehem, whom we love and adore, come and take birth in our hearts.

Jesus, living in Mary, come and live in your servants.

FOR LENT

Spare, O Lord, spare your people and let not your wrath be upon us forever.

AT PENTECOST

O Holy Spirit, Love substantial and eternal, deign to enkindle my soul with more ardent love for the Holy Trinity.

FOR ANY SEASON

To the King of ages, immortal and invisible, the only God, be honor and glory forever and ever. Amen.

Holy, holy, holy Lord, God of Hosts, the heavens and the earth are full of your glory.

My God, grant that I may love you and let the only reward of my love be to love you more and more.

My God, I love you.

Blessed be the Name of the Lord!

My God, I give you thanks for what you give and for what you take away. Your will be done.

My God, make us to be of one mind in the truth and one heart in love.

Make my divided self whole and one, Blessed Three in One.

The real me with the real you.

O God, be merciful to me a sinner.

Vouchsafe, O Lord, this day to keep us without sin.

O God, you are all-powerful, make me a saint.

Holy God, holy Almighty, holy Immortal One, have mercy on us.

May I receive your Word as Mary received your Word.

Hail, wounded Heart of our Redeemer! You are the image of the Heart of God the Father.

As you are in the Heart of the Father, Lord Jesus, let me be in your Heart.

Spirit, lead me to Christ.

Come, Holy Spirit, descend from the mind to the heart to the Christ-center of my life.

Jesus, Mary, and Joseph, I place all my trust in you.

Jesus, Mary, and Joseph, may I breathe out my soul in peace with you.

PRAYERS TO OUR BLESSED MOTHER

O Mary, Mother of God and Mother of Mercy, pray for us.

Mary, my Mother, keep me from sin.

Our Lady of Pure Love [or any other title], pray for us.

Mother of Mercy, our life, our sweetness, and our hope.

Queen of the Americas, pray for us.

Mother of love, of sorrow, and of mercy, pray for us.

My Mother, my hope.

Show yourself a Mother.

You are my Mother, O Virgin Mary. Keep me safe lest I ever offend your Son and obtain the grace I need to please him always and in all things.

Mary, Mother, Mediatrix of all graces, pray for me.

Blessed are you among women.

O Mary, make me to live in God, with God, and for God.

O Mary, Mother of Grace and Mother of mercy, protect us from our sinfulness and receive us at the hour of death.

O Mary, conceived without sin, pray for us who have recourse to you.

—from the Miraculous Medal

Lovely Lady dressed in blue, teach me how to pray. God was your little Child and you know the way.

Bless us, Mary, maiden mild; bless, too, her tender Child.

Mother of joy, sorrow, and glory, pray for us.

15

❧ ❖ ❧

Methods of Prayer

There are in our very rich Christian tradition and heritage, besides many beautiful prayers, some simple methods of prayer. These methods invite us to move beyond vocal prayer or the devout formulation of our prayer in words to a deeper communion with God. They invite us to enter more deeply into the revelations of God's love for us and to respond to that love with the silent but powerful yearnings of our hearts. They make space for the Holy Spirit to pray within us.

SCRIPTURAL PRAYER

It is well to keep the Sacred Scriptures enthroned in our home in a place of honor as a real presence of the Word in our midst.

1. Take the Sacred Text with reverence and call upon the Holy Spirit.

2. For ten minutes (or longer, if you are so drawn) listen to the Lord speaking to you through the Text, and respond to him.

3. At the end of the time, choose a word or phrase (perhaps one will have been "given" to you) to take with you, and thank the Lord for being with you and speaking to you.

For Scriptural Prayer any part of the Bible may be chosen. Some like to use the readings assigned by the Lectionary for reading at the particular day's Mass. Others like to follow the Bible through, taking each day that portion which is sufficient to nourish them. Others like to open the Bible randomly after calling upon the Holy Spirit to guide them—this is fine so long as there is no superstition attached to it.

Usually we do well to begin with the New Testament, especially the Gospels. Saint John's chapters on the Last Supper are especially deep and meaningful: John 13–17. Matthew's reporting of the Sermon on the Mount is another favorite that is most fruitful: Matthew 5–7. The Psalms are another favorite book of the Bible. A combination, beginning with some Gospel reading and then concluding with a single Psalm, might be very good.

Before using the Epistles for Scriptural

Prayer it might be well to read them as letters in the context of the Acts of the Apostles. Read the Acts through and as you encounter Paul's evangelization of the particular churches, stop and read the Epistle(s) to the church. Read it as a letter, read it right through, getting the whole sense of the Epistle as a letter from your revered teacher.

Whatever order you choose, do not be overly concerned about it, but rather be concerned simply to hear the Lord speaking to you through his inspired Word, speaking to your heart.

THE JESUS PRAYER

The Jesus Prayer has prevailed more among Eastern Christians and has its complement in the Centering Prayer in the West.

The disciple would go to his or her spiritual father or mother and ask for a "word of life." The one that became most common and popular is drawn from two Gospel events: the publican in the temple and the blind man at Jericho. It has been formulated variously but is basically this:

Lord Jesus Christ, Son of the Living God, have mercy on me a sinner.

The development of this Prayer usually requires the discerning help of a spiritual guide.

At first, the Prayer is said a certain number of times—perhaps a hundred—morning and evening, standing before an icon of Christ the Lord. A prayer cord or knotted rope is used to count the prayers. With each prayer one bows, or touches the floor, or prostrates on the knees and knuckles. As much as possible practitioners seek to continue the Prayer through the day and at night as they fall into sleep.

The Prayer is simplified as one aspect or another emerges into consciousness (here the discernment with a guide is most helpful). It may become for a time: "Lord, be merciful to me a sinner," and then: "Jesus, Son of God," as the pray-er becomes more aware of self as a sinner or of Jesus' glory, and so forth. In time it simplifies itself to the one sole word: "Jesus." The bodily participation might also simplify, till one stands, sits, or prostrates restfully and attentively throughout the assigned period of prayer. With time the Prayer tends to become more and more constant through the day and night. Gentleness and no forcing are most important. Communion with Jesus-God is the important thing—not the Prayer.

Anyone may feel free to use the Jesus

Prayer as a simple aspiration at any time and place.

> *Lord Jesus Christ, Son of the Living God, have mercy on me a sinner.*

THE STATIONS OF THE CROSS

If we are not able to go to a place where the Stations of the Cross have been erected, we can hold in our hands or look upon a crucifix that has been blessed for the purpose and mentally move from station to station. At each station we pray:

We adore you, O Christ, and we praise you,
Because by your holy Cross you have
   redeemed the world.

We then reflect on the appropriate scene from the Passion of Christ:

1. Jesus is condemned to death.
2. Jesus bears his cross.
3. Jesus falls the first time.
4. Jesus meets his Mother.
5. Jesus is helped by Simon.
6. Veronica wipes Jesus' face.

7. Jesus falls a second time.

8. Jesus consoles the weeping women.

9. Jesus falls the third time.

10. Jesus is stripped of his garments.

11. Jesus is nailed to the cross.

12. Jesus dies on the cross.

13. Jesus is taken down from the cross.

14. Jesus is laid in the tomb.

[15.] Jesus rises on the third day.

After reflecting on the scene for howsoever long we wish, we conclude the station with a prayer. It may be a prayer we compose from our own reflections or we might say the Lord's Prayer, the Hail Mary, and the Doxology.

THE ROSARY

When we pray the Rosary it is well to have in hand some beads which have been blessed for this purpose, to count the prayers and focus our attention. If we do not have beads, we can use our fingers.

We begin with the Sign of the Cross. The Apostles' Creed is said on the crucifix; the

Lord's Prayer is said on the larger or separate beads, the Hail Mary on the other beads, and the Doxology after each group of Hail Marys. Thus we say the Apostles' Creed, the Lord's Prayer, three Hail Marys, and a Doxology before beginning the decades. Each decade has the Lord's Prayer, ten Hail Marys, and a Doxology. After each Doxology we may add: "O my God, forgive us our sins, save us from the fires of hell, lead all souls to heaven, especially the most abandoned."

As we pray each decade, we meditate on one of fifteen mysteries or events from the lives of Jesus and Mary. It is traditional to pray five decades of the Rosary at a time. The first five mysteries are considered on Mondays and Thursdays and the Sundays of Advent; the second five on Tuesdays and Fridays and the Sundays of Lent; and the final mysteries on Wednesdays, Saturdays, and the other Sundays of the year. The mysteries of the Rosary are:

The Five Joyful Mysteries

1. The Annunciation

> The angel Gabriel as God's messenger asks Mary to become the mother of God and she accepts.

2. The Visitation

Mary goes to assist her cousin who is bearing John the Baptist.

3. The Nativity

Jesus is born in a stable in Bethlehem.

4. The Presentation

Jesus is presented in the Temple forty days after his birth and Simeon foretells his Passion.

5. The Finding of Jesus in the Temple

Mary and Joseph find Jesus after three days' searching.

The Five Sorrowful Mysteries

6. The Agony in the Garden

Jesus sweats blood as he takes on our sin.

7. The Scourging at the Pillar

Jesus is brutally scourged by the Roman soldiers.

8. The Crowning with Thorns

Jesus is mocked as a false King.

9. The Carrying of the Cross

Jesus carries his cross to Calvary.

10. **The Crucifixion**

   Jesus dies on the cross.

The Five Glorious Mysteries

11. **The Resurrection**

   Jesus rises from the dead on the third day.

12. **The Ascension**

   Jesus ascends into heaven on the fortieth day after his resurrection.

13. **The Descent of the Holy Spirit**

   The Holy Spirit comes upon Mary and the disciples ten days after Jesus ascended into heaven.

14. **The Assumption**

   The Blessed Virgin Mary is taken body and soul into heaven.

15. **The Coronation**

   The Blessed Virgin is crowned as Queen of Heaven and Earth.

At the end of the Rosary we say the Hail, Holy Queen (above, p. 48), adding:

Pray for us, Holy Mother of God,
That we may be worthy of the promises of
　Christ.

Let us pray.

O God, whose only begotten Son, by his life, death, and resurrection, has purchased for us the rewards of eternal life, we pray you, grant that we, who meditate upon these mysteries of the most holy Rosary of the Blessed Virgin Mary, may imitate what they contain and obtain what they promise through the same Christ, our Lord. Amen.

CENTERING PRAYER

Centering Prayer is a modern name, deriving from Thomas Merton, for an ancient method of prayer coming from the same source as the Jesus Prayer. It was brought to the West by Saint John Cassian in the early fifth century. It presupposes that Gospel Prayer and other forms of prayer have brought us to the point where we are desirous, in faith, simply to be with God in love. The method is very simple.

Sit comfortably in a chair that will give your back good support, and gently close your eyes. It is well to choose a place where you will not be disturbed by any sudden intrusion. A quiet place is helpful, though not necessary.

1. At the beginning of the Prayer take a minute or two to quiet down and then move in faith and love to God dwelling in the depths of your being.

2. After resting for a bit in the center in faith-filled love, take up a single, simple word that expresses your being to God and let this word be gently present, directing you to the Presence, to God in you.

3. Whenever in the course of the Prayer you become aware of anything else, simply return to the Presence by gently using your prayer word.

4. At the end of your Prayer (we recommend a twenty-minute period, if possible) take a couple of minutes to come out of the Prayer, slowly praying the Our Father or some other favorite prayer.

Further teaching on this method of prayer may be found in the Image paperbacks *Daily We Touch Him* and *Centering Prayer*.

Saint Anne, pray for us.

NOTES

(We provide some pages here for you to write down some of your own favorite prayers not included in this collection.)